Stir Fry Cooking

Ninth edition

By Don Orwell

http://SuperfoodsToday.com

Your Free Gift

As a way of saying thanks for your purchase, I'm offering you my FREE eBook that is exclusive to my book and blog readers.

Superfoods Cookbook - Book Two has over 70 Superfoods recipes and complements Superfoods Cookbook Book One and it contains Superfoods Salads, Superfoods Smoothies and Superfoods Deserts with ultra-healthy non-refined ingredients. All ingredients are 100% Superfoods.

It also contains Superfoods Reference book which is organized by Superfoods (more than 60 of them, with the list of their benefits), Superfoods spices, all vitamins, minerals and antioxidants. Superfoods Reference Book lists Superfoods that can help with 12 diseases and 9 types of cancer.

http://www.SuperfoodsToday.com/FREE

Table of Contents

Introduction

Hello,

My name is Don Orwell and I had some life changing experiences in 2009 and that led me to start rethinking my eating habits and my current lifestyle. I have written a bunch of Superfoods related books (Superfoods Diet, Smart Carbs Detox, Superfoods Cookbook, a few books with Smoothies recipes, Superfoods Salads, Nighttime Eater, Superfoods Body Care etc.) and finally I have decided to expand my stir fry recipes collection and publish a Superfoods Sir Fry book. All ingredients in all recipes are 100% Superfoods. Enjoy!!

Superfoods Stir Fry Recipes

Allergy labels: SF – Soy Free, GF – Gluten Free, DF – Dairy Free, EF – Egg Free, V - Vegan, NF – Nut Free

Superfoods Stir Fry Marinade

This marinade has 100% Superfoods ingredients and it's great with any meat or fish and even veggies. Sesame oil and sesame seeds are Superfoods, just like ginger, garlic, scallions, black pepper and red hot chili flakes. I personally don't use soy at all and I replaced soy sauce with fish sauce but you can use soy sauce if you want. Red wine is also Superfood rich in anthocyanidins, quercetin and resveratrol.

- 3 tbsp. fish sauce - optional soy sauce
- 2 tsp. sesame oil
- 1 tsp. freshly grated ginger
- 1 garlic clove, diced
- 1/4 cup red wine or chicken broth or both

Optional:
- 1 Tbsp. arrowroot flour - if you want your stir fry thicker
- 1/4 cup chopped scallions
- 1 tsp. chili flakes (adjust for heat)
- 1/2 tsp. ground black pepper

Korean Spicy Stir Fry Marinade

- 3 tbsp. fish sauce - optional soy sauce
- 1 tsp. sesame oil
- 1 tsp. freshly grated ginger
- 1 garlic clove, diced
- 1 tsp. chili flakes or powder (adjust for heat)

Pork, Bok Choy & Celery Stir Fry

Serves 2 - Allergies: SF, GF, DF, EF, NF

- **10** o.z. Lean Pork Tenderloin
- **2** cups Bok Choy
- **1 cup** chopped celery
- **1** tsp coconut oil

Marinade pork in a Superfoods marinade. Stir fry drained pork in coconut oil and when it's no longer pink add celery and stir fry for 1 more minute. Add bok choy and stir fry for a minute longer and then add the rest of the marinade and stir fry for one more minute.

Nutrition Facts

Serving Size 574 g

Amount Per Serving

Calories 316	Calories from Fat 39

	% Daily Value*
Total Fat 4.3g	**7%**
Saturated Fat 1.1g	**6%**
Trans Fat 0.0g	
Cholesterol 82mg	**27%**
Sodium 1156mg	**48%**
Potassium 1314mg	**38%**
Total Carbohydrates 34.6g	**12%**
Dietary Fiber 8.8g	**35%**
Sugars 8.8g	
Protein 34.5g	

Vitamin A 33%	•	Vitamin C 81%
Calcium 9%	•	Iron 30%

Nutrition Grade A

* Based on a 2000 calorie diet

Lemon Chicken Stir Fry

Serves 3-4

Ingredients - Allergies: SF, GF, DF, EF, NF

- 1 lemon
- 1/2 cup chicken broth
- 3 tbsp. fish sauce
- 2 teaspoons arrowroot flour
- 1 tbsp. oil
- 1 pound boneless, skinless chicken breasts, trimmed and cut into 1-inch pieces
- 10 ounces mushrooms, halved or quartered
- 2 cups snow peas, stems and strings removed
- 1 bunch scallions, cut into 1-inch pieces, white and green parts divided
- 1 tbsp. chopped garlic

Instructions

Grate 1 tsp. lemon zest. Juice the lemon and mix 3 tbsp. of the juice with broth, fish sauce and arrowroot flour in a small bowl.

Heat oil in a skillet over high heat. Add chicken and cook, stirring occasionally, until just cooked through. Transfer to a plate. Add mushrooms to the pan and cook until the mushrooms are tender. Add snow peas, garlic, scallion whites and the lemon zest. Cook, stirring, around 30 seconds. Add the broth to the pan and cook, stirring, 2 to 3 minutes. Add scallion greens and the chicken and any accumulated juices and stir.

Pan seared Brussels sprouts

Serves 2

Ingredients - Allergies: SF, GF, DF, EF, NF

- 6 oz. cubed pork

- 2 tbsp. oil

- 1 pound Brussels sprouts, halved

- 1/2 large onion, chopped

- Salt and ground black pepper

Instructions

Cook pork in a skillet over high heat. Remove to a plate and chop. In same pan with pork fat, add coconut oil over high heat. Add onions and Brussels sprouts and cook, stirring occasionally, until sprouts are golden brown. Season with salt and pepper, to taste, and put pork back into pan. Serve immediately.

Beef and Broccoli Stir Fry

Serves 2 - Allergies: SF, GF, DF, EF, NF

- 10 o.z. Beef
- 2 cups Broccoli
- 1 tsp coconut oil

Marinade beef in a Superfoods marinade. Stir fry drained beef in coconut oil and when it's no longer pink add broccoli and stir fry for 2 more minutes. Add the rest of the marinade and stir fry for a minute. Serve with brown rice or quinoa.

Nutrition Facts

Serving Size 251 g

Amount Per Serving

Calories 342 — Calories from Fat 124

	% Daily Value*
Total Fat 13.8g	21%
Saturated Fat 4.0g	20%
Trans Fat 0.0g	
Cholesterol 127mg	42%
Sodium 1024mg	43%
Potassium 884mg	25%
Total Carbohydrates 7.0g	2%
Dietary Fiber 2.4g	10%
Sugars 1.7g	
Protein 46.5g	

Vitamin A 11%	•	Vitamin C 131%
Calcium 5%	•	Iron 154%

Nutrition Grade A-

* Based on a 2000 calorie diet

Garbanzo Stir Fry

Serves 2

Ingredients - Allergies: SF, GF, DF, EF, V, NF

- 2 tbsp. oil
- 1 tbsp. oregano
- 1 tbsp. chopped basil
- 1 clove garlic, crushed
- ground black pepper to taste
- 2 cups cooked garbanzo beans

- 1 large zucchini, halved and sliced
- 1/2 cup sliced mushrooms
- 1 tbsp. chopped cilantro
- 1 tomato, chopped

Heat oil in a skillet over medium heat. Stir in oregano, basil, garlic and pepper. Add the garbanzo beans and zucchini, stirring well to coat with oil and herbs. Cook for 10 minutes, stirring occasionally. Stir in mushrooms and cilantro; cook 10 minutes, stirring occasionally. Place the chopped tomato on top of the mixture to steam. Cover and cook 5 minutes more.

Thai Basil Chicken

Serves 1

Ingredients - Allergies: SF, GF, DF, NF

For the egg

- 1 egg
- 2 tbsp. of coconut oil for frying

Basil chicken

- 1 chicken breast (or any other cut of boneless chicken, about 200 grams)
- 5 cloves of garlic
- 4 Thai chilies
- 1 tbsp. oil for frying
- Fish sauce
- 1 handful of Thai holy basil leaves

Instructions

First, fry the egg.

Basil chicken

Cut the chicken into small pieces. Peel the garlic and chilies, and chop them fine. Add basil leaves.

Add about 1 tbsp. of oil to the pan.

When the oil is hot, add the chilies and garlic. Stir fry for half a minute.

Toss in your chicken and keep stir frying. Add fish sauce.

Add basil into the pan, fold it into the chicken, and turn off the heat.

Shrimp with Snow Peas

Serves 4.

Ingredients - Allergies: SF, GF, DF, EF, NF

Marinade

- 2 teaspoons arrowroot flour
- 1 Tbsp red wine
- 1/2 tsp. salt

Stir Fry

- 1 pound shrimp, peeled and deveined
- 2 Tbsp oil
- 1 Tbsp minced ginger
- 3 garlic cloves, sliced thinly
- 1/2 pound snow peas, strings removed
- 2 teaspoons fish sauce
- 1/4 cup chicken broth
- 4 green onions, white and light green parts, sliced diagonally
- 2 teaspoons dark roasted sesame oil

Instructions

Mix all the ingredients for the marinade in a bowl and then add the shrimp. Mix to coat. Let it marinade 15 minutes while you prepare the peas, ginger, and garlic.

25 | P a g e

Add the coconut oil in the wok and let it get hot. Add the garlic and ginger and combine. Stir-fry for about 30 seconds.

Add the marinade to the wok, add the snow peas, fish sauce and chicken broth. Stir-fry until the shrimp turns pink. Add the green onions and stir-fry for one more minute. Turn off the heat and add the sesame oil. Toss once more and serve with steamed brown rice or soba gluten free noodles.

Pork and Green Beans Stir Fry
Serves 1 - Allergies: SF, GF, DF, EF, NF

- 6oz. of lean Pork

- 1 cup of Green Beans, snapped in half. Use as much veggies as you want or replace Green beans with Kale.

- 1 garlic clove, chopped

- 1/2 inch of peeled and chopped ginger

- Season with fish sauce.

Nutrition Facts

Serving Size 285 g

Amount Per Serving

Calories 317	Calories from Fat 97

	% Daily Value*
Total Fat 10.8g	17%
Saturated Fat 2.7g	14%
Trans Fat 0.1g	
Cholesterol 124mg	41%
Sodium 104mg	4%
Potassium 946mg	27%
Total Carbohydrates 7.8g	3%
Dietary Fiber 3.7g	15%
Sugars 1.5g	
Protein 46.5g	

Vitamin A 15%	•	Vitamin C 30%
Calcium 5%	•	Iron 17%

Nutrition Grade A
* Based on a 2000 calorie diet

Cashew chicken

Serves 4

Ingredients - Allergies: SF, GF, DF, EF, NF

- 1 bunch scallions
- 1 pound skinless boneless chicken thighs
- 1/2 tsp. salt
- 1/4 tsp. black pepper
- 3 tbsp. oil
- 1 red bell pepper and 1 stalk of celery, chopped
- 4 garlic cloves, finely chopped
- 1 1/2 tbsp. finely chopped peeled fresh ginger
- 1/4 tsp. dried hot red-pepper flakes
- 3/4 cup chicken broth
- 1 1/2 tbsp. fish sauce
- 1 1/2 teaspoons arrowroot flour
- 1/2 cup salted roasted whole cashews

Instructions

Chop scallions and separate green and white parts. Pat chicken dry and cut into 3/4-inch pieces and season with salt and pepper. Heat a wok or a skillet over high heat. Add oil and then stir-fry chicken until cooked through, 3 to 4 minutes. Transfer to a plate. Add garlic, bell pepper, celery, ginger, red-pepper flakes, and scallion whites to wok and stir-fry until peppers are just tender, 4 to 5 minutes.

Mix together broth, fish sauce and arrowroot flour, then stir into vegetables in wok. Reduce heat and simmer, stirring occasionally, until thickened. Stir in cashews, scallion greens, and chicken along with any juices.

Bass Celery Tomato Bok Choy Stir Fry
Serves 2

Ingredients - Allergies: SF, GF, DF, EF

- 1/2 pound bass fillets
- 1 cup Celery
- 1/2 cup sliced Tomatoes
- 1/2 cup sliced Bok Choy
- 1/2 cup sliced carrots and cucumbers
- 1 Tsp. oil

Instructions

Marinade bass in a Superfoods marinade. Stir fry drained bass in coconut oil for few minutes, add all vegetables and stir fry for 2 more minutes. Add the rest of the marinade and stir fry for a minute. Serve with brown rice or quinoa.

Broccoli, Yellow Peppers & Beef Stir Fry

Serves 2

Ingredients - Allergies: SF, GF, DF, EF

- 1/2 pound beef
- 1 cup Broccoli
- 1/2 cup sliced Yellow Peppers
- 1/2 cup chopped onions
- 1 Tbsp. sesame seeds
- 1 Tsp. oil

Instructions

Marinade beef in a Superfoods marinade. Stir fry drained beef in coconut oil for few minutes, add all vegetables and stir fry for 2 more minutes. Add the rest of the marinade and stir fry for a minute. Serve with brown rice or quinoa.

Chinese Celery, Mushrooms & Fish Stir Fry

Serves 2

Ingredients - Allergies: SF, GF, DF, EF

- 1/2 pound fish fillets
- 1 cup Chinese Celery
- 1 cup Mushrooms sliced in half
- 1/2 cup peppers sliced diagonally
- 1 Tsp. oil

Instructions

Marinade fish in a Superfoods marinade. Stir fry drained fish in coconut oil for few minutes, add all vegetables and stir fry for 2 more minutes. Add the rest of the marinade and stir fry for a minute. Serve with brown rice or quinoa.

Pork, Green Pepper and Tomato Stir Fry

Serves 2

Ingredients - Allergies: SF, GF, DF, EF

- 1/2 pound cubed pork
- 1 cup Green Peppers
- 1/2 cup sliced Tomatoes
- 1 tsp. ground black pepper
- 1 Tsp. oil

Instructions
Marinade pork in a Superfoods marinade. Stir fry drained pork in coconut oil for few minutes, add all vegetables and stir fry for 2 more minutes. Add the rest of the marinade and stir fry for a minute. Serve with brown rice or quinoa.

Pork, Red & Green Peppers, Onion & Carrots Stir Fry
Serves 2

Ingredients - Allergies: SF, GF, DF, EF

- 1/2 pound cubed pork
- 1/2 cup chopped Red Peppers
- 1/2 cup chopped Green Peppers
- 1/2 cup sliced onion
- 1/2 cup sliced carrots
- 1 Tsp. oil

Instructions

Marinade pork in a Superfoods marinade. Stir fry drained pork in coconut oil for few minutes, add all vegetables and stir fry for 2 more minutes. Add the rest of the marinade and stir fry for a minute. Serve with brown rice or quinoa.

Chicken Edamame Stir Fry

Serves 2

Ingredients - Allergies: SF, GF, DF, EF

- 1/2 pound chicken
- 1 cup Edamame pre-cooked in boiling water for 3 minutes
- 1/2 cup sliced carrots
- 1 Tsp. oil

Instructions
Marinade chicken in a Superfoods marinade. Stir fry drained chicken in coconut oil for few minutes, add all vegetables and stir fry for 2 more minutes. Add the rest of the marinade and stir fry for a minute. Serve with brown rice or quinoa.

Chicken, Zucchini, Carrots and Baby Corn Stir Fry
Serves 2

Ingredients - Allergies: SF, GF, DF, EF

- 1/2 pound chicken
- 1 cup Zucchini
- 1/2 cup sliced Carrots
- 1/2 cup Baby Corn
- 1 Tbsp. chopped Cilantro
- 1 Tsp. oil

Instructions
Marinade chicken in a Superfoods marinade. Stir fry drained chicken in coconut oil for few minutes, add all vegetables and stir fry for 2 more minutes. Add the rest of the marinade and stir fry for a minute. Serve with brown rice or quinoa over bed of lettuce.

Vegan Stir Fry

Serves 2

Ingredients - Allergies: SF, GF, DF, EF, V

- 1/2 pound shiitake mushrooms
- 1/2 cup Chinese Celery
- 1/2 cup sliced carrots and cucumbers
- 1 Tsp. oil

Instructions

Marinade mushrooms in a Superfoods marinade. Stir fry drained mushrooms in coconut oil for few minutes, add all other vegetables and stir fry for 2 more minutes. Add the rest of the marinade and stir fry for a minute. Serve with brown rice or quinoa.

Eggplant, Chinese Celery & Peppers Stir Fry
Serves 2

Ingredients - Allergies: SF, GF, DF, EF, V

- 1/2 pound cubed eggplant
- 1/2 cup Chinese Celery
- 1/2 cup sliced Red Peppers
- 1/4 cup sliced chili Peppers
- 1 Tsp. oil

Instructions

Marinade eggplant in a Superfoods marinade. Stir fry drained eggplant in coconut oil for few minutes, add all vegetables and stir fry for 2 more minutes. Add the rest of the marinade and stir fry for a minute. Serve with brown rice or quinoa.

Pork Fried Brown Rice

Serves 2

Ingredients - Allergies: SF, GF, DF, EF

- 1/2 pound cubed pork
- 1 cup Peppers
- 1/2 cup sliced Carrots
- 1 Tbsp. black sesame seeds
- 1 cup cooked brown rice
- 1 Tsp. oil

Instructions

Marinade pork in a Superfoods marinade. Stir fry drained pork in coconut oil for few minutes, add all vegetables and stir fry for 2 more minutes. Add the rest of the marinade and stir fry for a minute. Stir in brown rice and black sesame seeds.

Chicken, Red Peppers, Zucchini & Cashews Stir Fry
Serves 2

Ingredients - Allergies: SF, GF, DF, EF

- 1/2 pound chicken
- 1 cup Zucchini
- 1/2 cup sliced Red Peppers
- 1/2 cup sliced scallions
- 1/4 cup Cashews
- 1 Tsp. oil

Instructions

Marinade chicken in a Superfoods marinade. Stir fry drained chicken in coconut oil for few minutes, add all vegetables and stir fry for 2 more minutes. Add the rest of the marinade and stir fry for a minute. Serve with brown rice or quinoa.

Shrimp, Asparagus, Broccoli & Carrots Stir Fry

Serves 2

Ingredients - Allergies: SF, GF, DF, EF

- 1/2 pound shrimp and calamari mix
- 1/2 cup Asparagus
- 1/2 cup sliced Carrots
- 1/2 cup sliced Broccoli
- 1/2 cup sliced Chinese celery, baby corn and mushrooms
- 1 Tsp. oil

Instructions

Marinade shrimp in a Superfoods marinade. Stir fry drained shrimp in coconut oil for few minutes, add all vegetables and stir fry for 2 more minutes. Add the rest of the marinade and stir fry for a minute. Serve with brown rice or quinoa.

Chicken, Carrots & Snow Peas Stir Fry
Serves 2

Ingredients - Allergies: SF, GF, DF, EF

- 1/2 pound chicken
- 1 cup Carrots
- 1 cup Snow Peas
- 1 Tsp. oil

Instructions

Marinade chicken in a Superfoods marinade. Stir fry drained chicken in coconut oil for few minutes, add all vegetables and stir fry for 2 more minutes. Add the rest of the marinade and stir fry for a minute. Serve with brown rice or quinoa.

Calamari, Shrimp & Bok Choy Stir Fry

Serves 2

Ingredients - Allergies: SF, GF, DF, EF

- 1 cup shrimp
- 1 cup Calamari
- 1 cup sliced Bok Choy
- 1 Tsp. oil

Instructions

Marinade calamari and shrimp in a Superfoods marinade. Stir fry drained calamari & shrimp in coconut oil for few minutes, add bok choy and stir fry for 2 more minutes. Add the rest of the marinade and stir fry for a minute. Serve with brown rice or quinoa.

Beef Liver, Chinese Celery & Mushrooms Stir Fry
Serves 2

Ingredients - Allergies: SF, GF, DF, EF

- 1/2 pound beef liver
- 1 cup Chinese Celery
- 1 cup Mushrooms
- 1 Tsp. oil

Instructions
Marinade beef liver in a Superfoods marinade. Stir fry drained beef liver in coconut oil for few minutes, add all vegetables and stir fry for 2 more minutes. Add the rest of the marinade and stir fry for a minute. Serve with brown rice or quinoa.

Chicken, Green beans & Carrot Stir Fry

Serves 2

Ingredients - Allergies: SF, GF, DF, EF

- 1/2 pound chicken
- 1 cup Green Beans
- 1/2 cup chopped Carrot
- 1 Tbsp. Chia seeds
- 1 Tsp. oil

Instructions

Marinade chicken in a Superfoods marinade. Stir fry drained chicken in coconut oil for few minutes, add all vegetables and stir fry for 2 more minutes. Add the rest of the marinade and stir fry for a minute. Serve with brown rice or quinoa.

Mixed Seafood, Spinach & Red Peppers Stir Fry
Serves 2

Ingredients - Allergies: SF, GF, DF, EF

- 1/2 pound mixed seafood
- 1 cup Spinach
- 1 cup sliced Red Peppers
- 1/2 cup chopped scallions
- 1 Tsp. oil

Instructions

Marinade seafood in a Superfoods marinade. Stir fry drained mixed seafood in coconut oil for few minutes, add red peppers and stir fry for 2 more minutes. Add the rest of the marinade and spinach and stir fry for a minute. Serve with brown rice or quinoa.

Squid, Asparagus and Red Peppers Stir Fry
Serves 2

Ingredients - Allergies: SF, GF, DF, EF

- 1/2 pound squid
- 1 cup Asparagus
- 1 cup Red Peppers
- 1 Tbsp. sesame seeds
- 1 Tsp. oil

Instructions

Marinade squid in a Superfoods marinade. Stir fry drained squid and asparagus in coconut oil for few minutes, add all other ingredients and stir fry for 2 more minutes. Add the rest of the marinade and stir fry for a minute. Serve with brown rice or quinoa.

Shrimp, Squid, Red Peppers & Green Peppers Stir Fry
Serves 2

Ingredients - Allergies: SF, GF, DF, EF

- 1/4 pound shrimp
- 1/4 pound squid
- 1 cup Red peppers
- 1 cup Green peppers
- 1/4 cup Basil leaves
- 1 Tsp. oil

Instructions

Marinade shrimp and squid in a Superfoods marinade. Stir fry drained shrimp and squid in coconut oil for few minutes, add all vegetables and stir fry for 2 more minutes. Add the rest of the marinade and stir fry for a minute. Serve with brown rice or quinoa.

Bitter Gourd, Shrimp & Peppers Stir Fry

Serves 2

Ingredients - Allergies: SF, GF, DF, EF

- 1/2 pound shrimp
- 1 cup chopped Bitter Gourd pre-cooked for 2 minutes in boiling water
- 1/2 cup sliced Red peppers
- 1/4 cup Cashews
- 1 Tsp. oil

Instructions

Marinade shrimp in a Superfoods marinade. Stir fry drained shrimp and bitter gourd in coconut oil for few minutes, add all vegetables and stir fry for 2 more minutes. Add the rest of the marinade and stir fry for a minute. Serve with brown rice or quinoa.

Pork, Mushrooms & Basil Stir Fry
Serves 2

Ingredients - Allergies: SF, GF, DF, EF

- 1/2 pound cubed pork
- 1 cup sliced mushrooms
- 1/2 cup Basil leaves
- 1/2 cup sliced carrots and cucumbers
- 1 Tsp. oil

Instructions

Marinade beef in a Superfoods marinade. Stir fry drained bass in coconut oil for few minutes, add all vegetables and stir fry for 2 more minutes. Add the rest of the marinade and stir fry for a minute. Serve with brown rice or quinoa.

Green Superfoods Stir Fry

Serves 2

Ingredients - Allergies: SF, GF, DF, EF

- 1/2 cup Kale
- 1/2 cup Chinese Celery
- 1/2 cup shiitake Mushrooms
- 1/2 cup sliced Bok Choy
- 1/2 cup Asparagus
- 1 Tsp. oil

Instructions

Marinade Asparagus and Kale in a Superfoods marinade. Stir fry drained Asparagus in coconut oil for few minutes, add all other vegetables and stir fry for 2 more minutes. Add the rest of the marinade and stir fry for a minute. Serve with brown rice or quinoa.

Pork Liver & Spinach Stir Fry

Serves 2

Ingredients - Allergies: SF, GF, DF, EF

- 1/2 pound cubed pork liver
- 1 cup Spinach Celery
- 1/2 cup sliced Onions
- 1 Tsp. oil

Instructions

Marinade pork liver in a Superfoods marinade. Stir fry drained liver in coconut oil for few minutes, add all vegetables and stir fry for 2 more minutes. Add the rest of the marinade and stir fry for a minute. Serve with brown rice or quinoa.

Squid, Shiitake Mushrooms & Basil Stir Fry

Serves 2

Ingredients - Allergies: SF, GF, DF, EF

- 1/2 pound squid
- 1 cup sliced Mushrooms
- 1/2 cup Basil leaves
- 1/2 cup sliced Bok Choy
- 1/2 cup sliced carrots and red pepers
- 1 Tsp. oil

Instructions

Marinade squid in a Superfoods marinade. Stir fry drained squid in coconut oil for few minutes, add all vegetables and stir fry for 2 more minutes. Add the rest of the marinade and stir fry for a minute. Serve with brown rice or quinoa.

Chicken, Onion & Carrot Stir Fry
Serves 2

Ingredients - Allergies: SF, GF, DF, EF

- 1/2 pound chicken
- 1 cup sliced onions
- 1/2 cup sliced Bok Choy
- 1/2 cup sliced carrots and Chinese Celery
- 1 Tsp. oil

Instructions

Marinade chicken in a Superfoods marinade. Stir fry drained chicken in coconut oil for few minutes, add all vegetables and stir fry for 2 more minutes. Add the rest of the marinade and stir fry for a minute. Serve with brown rice or quinoa.

Beef, Green beans, Broccoli & Carrot Stir Fry

Serves 2

Ingredients - Allergies: SF, GF, DF, EF

- 1/2 pound beef
- 1/2 cup chopped Broccoli
- 1/2 cup chopped Green beans
- 1/2 cup sliced carrots
- 1/2 cup Baby Corn
- 1 Tsp. oil

Instructions

Marinade beef in a Superfoods marinade. Stir fry drained beef in coconut oil for few minutes, add all vegetables and stir fry for 2 more minutes. Add the rest of the marinade and stir fry for a minute. Serve with brown rice or quinoa.

Pork, Onion & Bok Choy Stir Fry

Serves 2

Ingredients - Allergies: SF, GF, DF, EF

- 1/2 pound cubed pork
- 1/2 cup sliced onions
- 1 cup sliced Bok Choy
- 1/2 cup sliced Chinese Celery
- 1 Tsp. oil

Instructions

Marinade pork in a Superfoods marinade. Stir fry drained pork in coconut oil for few minutes, add all vegetables and stir fry for 2 more minutes. Add the rest of the marinade and stir fry for a minute. Serve with brown rice or quinoa.

Chicken, Red Peppers & Bok Choy Stir Fry

Serves 2

Ingredients - Allergies: SF, GF, DF, EF

- 1/2 pound chicken
- 1/2 cup sliced onions
- 1 cup sliced Bok Choy
- 1/2 cup sliced Red Peppers
- 1 Tsp. oil

Instructions

Marinade chicken in a Superfoods marinade. Stir fry drained chicken in coconut oil for few minutes, add all vegetables and stir fry for 2 more minutes. Add the rest of the marinade and stir fry for a minute. Serve with brown rice or quinoa.

Chicken, Eggplant & Red Peppers Stir Fry

Serves 2

Ingredients - Allergies: SF, GF, DF, EF

- 1/2 pound chicken
- 1 cup sliced Eggplant
- 1/2 cup sliced Mushrooms
- 1 cup sliced Red peppers
- 1 Tsp. oil

Instructions

Marinade chicken in a Superfoods marinade. Stir fry drained chicken in coconut oil for few minutes, add all vegetables and stir fry for 2 more minutes. Add the rest of the marinade and stir fry for a minute. Serve with brown rice or quinoa.

Pork, Cauliflower & Chinese Celery Stir Fry

Serves 2

Ingredients - Allergies: SF, GF, DF, EF

- 1/2 pound cubed pork
- 1/2 cup chopped Cauliflower
- 1/2 cup sliced Broccoli
- 1/2 cup sliced Red Peppers
- 1/2 cup sliced Chinese Celery
- 1 Tsp. oil

Instructions

Marinade pork in a Superfoods marinade. Stir fry drained pork in coconut oil for few minutes, add all vegetables and stir fry for 2 more minutes. Add the rest of the marinade and stir fry for a minute. Serve with brown rice or quinoa.

Chicken, Onion & Green & Red Peppers Stir Fry
Serves 2

Ingredients - Allergies: SF, GF, DF, EF

- 1/2 pound chicken
- 1/2 cup sliced onions
- 1/2 cup sliced Green Peppers
- 1/2 cup sliced Red Peppers
- 1/2 cup Cashews
- 1 Tsp. oil

Instructions

Marinade chicken in a Superfoods marinade. Stir fry drained chicken in coconut oil for few minutes, add all vegetables and stir fry for 2 more minutes. Add the rest of the marinade and stir fry for a minute. Serve with brown rice or quinoa.

Beef, Eggplant & Green Peppers Stir Fry

Serves 2

Ingredients - Allergies: SF, GF, DF, EF

- 1/2 pound beef
- 1 cup sliced Eggplants
- 1/2 cup sliced Green peppers
- 1/2 cup sliced carrots and Chinese Celery
- 1 Tsp. Coconut oil

Instructions

Marinade beef in a Superfoods marinade. Stir fry drained beef in coconut oil for few minutes, add all vegetables and stir fry for 2 more minutes. Add the rest of the marinade and stir fry for a minute. Serve with brown rice or quinoa.

Cauliflower & Shiitake Stir Fry

Serves 2

Ingredients - Allergies: SF, GF, DF, EF

- 2 cups Cauliflower
- 1 cup sliced Shiitake mushrooms
- 1/2 cup sliced Green beans
- 1/2 cup sliced Broccoli
- 1/2 cup sliced carrot
- 1 Tsp. Coconut oil

Instructions

Stir fry cauliflower and broccoli in coconut oil for few minutes, add carrots and green beans and stir fry for 2 more minutes. Add the mushrooms and stir fry for 3 minutes more. Serve with brown rice or quinoa.

Pork, Cabbage & Bok Choy Stir Fry

Serves 2

Ingredients - Allergies: SF, GF, DF, EF

- 1/2 pound cubed pork
- 1 cup sliced Chinese cabbage
- 1/2 cup sliced bok choy
- 1/2 cup sliced red peppers
- 1 Tsp. oil

Instructions

Marinade pork in a Superfoods marinade. Stir fry drained pork in coconut oil for few minutes, add all vegetables and stir fry for 2 more minutes. Add the rest of the marinade and stir fry for a minute. Serve with brown rice or quinoa.

Chicken & Chinese Celery Stir Fry

Serves 2

Ingredients - Allergies: SF, GF, DF, EF

- 1/2 pound chicken
- 2 cups sliced Chinese Celery
- 1 Tsp. oil

Instructions

Marinade chicken in a Superfoods marinade. Stir fry drained chicken in coconut oil for few minutes, add Chinese celery and stir fry for 2 more minutes. Add the rest of the marinade and stir fry for a minute. Serve with brown rice or quinoa.

Chicken, Broccoli & Carrots Stir Fry

Serves 2

Ingredients - Allergies: SF, GF, DF, EF

- 1/2 pound chicken
- 1 cup sliced Broccoli
- 1/2 cup sliced red peppers
- 1/2 cup sliced carrots
- 1 Tsp. oil

Instructions

Marinade chicken in a Superfoods marinade. Stir fry drained chicken in coconut oil for few minutes, add all vegetables and stir fry for 2 more minutes. Add the rest of the marinade and stir fry for a minute. Serve with brown rice or quinoa.

Chicken & Carrots Stir Fry
Serves 2

Ingredients - Allergies: SF, GF, DF, EF

- 1/2 pound chicken
- 2 cup sliced Carrots
- 1/2 cup sliced onions
- 1 Tsp. oil

Instructions

Marinade chicken in a Superfoods marinade. Stir fry drained chicken in coconut oil for few minutes, add all vegetables and stir fry for 2 more minutes. Add the rest of the marinade and stir fry for a minute. Serve with brown rice or quinoa.

Beef, Onions & Green & Red Peppers Stir Fry

Serves 2

Ingredients - Allergies: SF, GF, DF, EF

- 1/2 pound beef
- 1 cup sliced Onions
- 1/2 cup sliced Green & Red peppers
- 1/2 cup sliced carrots and Celery
- 1 Tsp. oil

Instructions

Marinade beef in a Superfoods marinade. Stir fry drained beef in coconut oil for few minutes, add all vegetables and stir fry for 2 more minutes. Add the rest of the marinade and stir fry for a minute. Serve with brown rice or quinoa.

Onions, Lentils & Tomatoes Stir Fry

Serves 2

Ingredients - Allergies: SF, GF, DF, EF

- 1/2 pound cooked lentis
- 1 cup sliced Onions
- 1/2 cup sliced parsley
- 1/2 cup sliced carrots and Celery
- 1 Tsp. oil

Instructions

Add all vegetables and stir fry for 2 more minutes. Add the lentils and stir fry for a minute. Serve with brown rice or quinoa.

Eggplant, Mushrooms & Carrots Stir Fry

Serves 2

Ingredients - Allergies: SF, GF, DF, EF

- 1/2 pound sliced Eggplant
- 1 cup sliced Mushrooms
- 1/4 cup Basil leaves
- 1/2 cup sliced carrots and red peppers
- 1 Tsp. oil

Instructions

Marinade eggplant in a Superfoods marinade. Stir fry drained eggplant in coconut oil for few minutes, add all vegetables and stir fry for 2 more minutes. Add the rest of the marinade and stir fry for a minute. Serve with brown rice or quinoa.

Chicken, Shiitake & Carrots Stir Fry

Serves 2

Ingredients - Allergies: SF, GF, DF, EF

- 1/2 pound chicken
- 1 cup sliced Shiitake mushrooms
- 1/2 cup sliced Leeks
- 1/2 cup sliced carrots and Celery
- 1 Tsp. oil

Instructions

Marinade chicken in a Superfoods marinade. Stir fry drained chicken in coconut oil for few minutes, add all vegetables and stir fry for 2 more minutes. Add the rest of the marinade and stir fry for a minute. Serve with brown rice or quinoa.

Chicken & Bok Choy Stir Fry

Serves 2

Ingredients - Allergies: SF, GF, DF, EF

- 1/2 pound chicken
- 2 cups sliced Bok Choy
- 1/2 cup sliced Onions
- 1 Tsp. oil

Instructions

Marinade chicken in a Superfoods marinade. Stir fry drained chicken in coconut oil for few minutes, add all vegetables and stir fry for 2 more minutes. Add the rest of the marinade and stir fry for a minute. Serve with brown rice or quinoa.

Shrimp & Bok Choy Stir Fry
Serves 2

Ingredients - Allergies: SF, GF, DF, EF

- 1/2 pound shrimp
- 2 cups sliced Bok Choy
- 1/2 cup sliced Green onions
- 1/2 cup sliced Chinese Celery
- 1 Tsp. oil

Instructions

Marinade shrimp in a Superfoods marinade. Stir fry drained shrimp in coconut oil for few minutes, add all vegetables and stir fry for 2 more minutes. Add the rest of the marinade and stir fry for a minute. Serve with brown rice or quinoa.

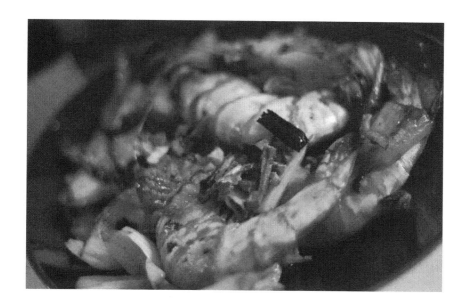

Chicken, Green Beeans & Red Peppers Stir Fry
Serves 2

Ingredients - Allergies: SF, GF, DF, EF

- 1/2 pound chicken
- 1 cup sliced Green Beans
- 1/2 cup sliced red peppers
- 1/2 cup sliced carrots and Celery
- 1 Tsp. oil

Instructions

Marinade chicken in a Superfoods marinade. Stir fry drained chicken in coconut oil for few minutes, add all vegetables and stir fry for 2 more minutes. Add the rest of the marinade and stir fry for a minute. Serve with brown rice or quinoa.

Squid & Kimchi Stir Fry
Serves 2

Ingredients - Allergies: SF, GF, DF, EF

- 1/2 pound squid
- 1 cup Kimchi
- 1/2 cup chopped green onions
- 1/4 cup chopped Cilantro
- 1 Tsp. oil

Instructions

Marinade squid in a Superfoods marinade mixed with kimchi liquid. Stir fry drained squid in coconut oil for few minutes, add all kimchi and green onions and stir fry for 2 more minutes. Add the rest of the marinade, cilantro and stir fry for a minute. Serve with brown rice or quinoa.

Pork, Scallions & Celery Stir Fry

Serves 2

Ingredients - Allergies: SF, GF, DF, EF

- 1/2 pound cubed pork
- 1 cup sliced scallions
- 1/2 cup sliced onions
- 1/2 cup sliced Celery
- 1 Tsp. oil

Instructions

Marinade pork in a Superfoods marinade. Stir fry drained pork in coconut oil for few minutes, add all vegetables and stir fry for 2 more minutes. Add the rest of the marinade and stir fry for a minute. Serve with brown rice or quinoa.

Squid & Bitter Melon Stir Fry

Serves 2

Ingredients - Allergies: SF, GF, DF, EF

- 1/2 pound squid
- 1 cup sliced Bitter Melon
- 1/2 cup sliced onions
- 1/2 cup sliced Celery
- 1 Tsp. oil

Instructions

Marinade squid in a Superfoods marinade. Stir fry drained squid in coconut oil for few minutes, add all vegetables and stir fry for 2 more minutes. Add the rest of the marinade and stir fry for a minute. Serve with brown rice or quinoa.

Shrimp, Bok Choy & Red Peppers Stir Fry

Serves 2

Ingredients - Allergies: SF, GF, DF, EF

- 1/2 pound shrimp
- 1 cup sliced Bok Choy
- 1/2 cup sliced red peppers
- 1/2 cup sliced red onions and mushrooms
- 1 Tsp. oil

Instructions

Marinade shrimp in a Superfoods marinade. Stir fry drained shrimp in coconut oil for few minutes, add all vegetables and stir fry for 2 more minutes. Add the rest of the marinade and stir fry for a minute. Serve with brown rice or quinoa.

Pork Liver, Green Beans & Zucchini Stir Fry
Serves 2

Ingredients - Allergies: SF, GF, DF, EF

- 1/2 pound cubed pork liver
- 1 cup sliced Green Beans
- 1/2 cup sliced zucchini
- 1/2 cup sliced Celery and few red chili peppers
- 1 Tsp. oil

Instructions

Marinade liver in a Superfoods marinade. Stir fry drained liver in coconut oil for few minutes, add all vegetables and stir fry for 2 more minutes. Add the rest of the marinade and stir fry for a minute. Serve with brown rice or quinoa.

Shrimp, Edamame & Oyster Mushrooms Stir Fry
Serves 2

Ingredients - Allergies: SF, GF, DF, EF

- 1/2 pound shrimp
- 1 cup shelled edamame
- 1/2 cup sliced red peppers
- 1 cup sliced oyster mushrooms
- 1 Tsp. oil

Instructions

Marinade shrimp in a Superfoods marinade. Stir fry drained shrimp in coconut oil for few minutes, add all vegetables and stir fry for 2 more minutes. Add the rest of the marinade and stir fry for a minute. Serve with brown rice or quinoa.

Pork & Mushrooms Stir Fry
Serves 2

Ingredients - Allergies: SF, GF, DF, EF

- 1/2 pound cubed pork
- 1 1/2 cup sliced mushroom
- 1 cup sliced onions
- 1 Tsp. oil

Instructions

Marinade pork in a Superfoods marinade. Stir fry drained pork in coconut oil for few minutes, add all vegetables and stir fry for 2 more minutes. Add the rest of the marinade and stir fry for a minute. Serve with brown rice or quinoa.

Shrimp, Broccoli & Water Chestnuts Stir Fry

Serves 2

Ingredients - Allergies: SF, GF, DF, EF

- 1/2 pound shrimp
- 1 cup sliced Broccoli
- 1/2 cup sliced water chestnuts
- 1/2 cup sliced Celery
- 1 Tsp. oil

Instructions

Marinade shrimp in a Superfoods marinade. Stir fry drained shrimp in coconut oil for few minutes, add all vegetables and stir fry for 2 more minutes. Add the rest of the marinade and stir fry for a minute. Serve with brown rice or quinoa.

Mixed Seafood, Chinese Celery & Yelllow Zucchini Stir Fry

Serves 2

Ingredients - Allergies: SF, GF, DF, EF

- 1/2 pound mixed seafood
- 1 cup sliced Chinese Celery
- 1/2 cup sliced bok choy
- 1/2 cup sliced onions and Celery
- 1 Tsp. oil

Instructions

Marinade seafood in a Superfoods marinade. Stir fry drained seafood in coconut oil for few minutes, add all vegetables and stir fry for 2 more minutes. Add the rest of the marinade and stir fry for a minute. Serve with brown rice or quinoa.

Pork, Cashews & Carrots Stir Fry
Serves 2

Ingredients - Allergies: SF, GF, DF, EF

- 1/2 pound cubed pork
- 1 cup sliced Green Pepper
- 1/2 cup sliced carrots
- 1/2 cup sliced onions
- 1/2 cup cashews
- 1 Tsp. oil

Instructions

Marinade pork in a Superfoods marinade. Stir fry drained pork in coconut oil for few minutes, add all vegetables and stir fry for 2 more minutes. Add the rest of the marinade and stir fry for a minute. Serve with brown rice or quinoa.

Asparagus, Sesame Beef & Red Peppers Stir Fry
Serves 2

Ingredients - Allergies: SF, GF, DF, EF

- 1/2 pound beef
- 1 cup sliced Red Pepper
- 1 cup sliced carrots
- 1/2 cup sliced onions
- 1/2 sesame seeds
- 1 Tsp. oil

Instructions

Marinade beef in a Superfoods marinade. Roll drained beef in sesame seeds and stir fry in coconut oil for few minutes with asparagus. Add other vegetables and stir fry for 4 more minutes. Add the rest of the marinade and stir fry for a minute. Serve with brown rice or quinoa.

Baby Corn, Mushrooms & Asparagus Stir Fry
Serves 2

Ingredients - Allergies: SF, GF, DF, EF

- 1 cup mushrooms
- 1/2 cup Baby corn
- 1/2 cup sliced green beans
- 1/2 cup sliced yellow peppers
- 1/2 cup asparagus
- 1 Tsp. oil

Instructions

Stir fry asparagus, green beans and baby corn in coconut oil for few minutes, add peppers and mushrooms and stir fry for 2 more minutes. Add the superfoods marinade and stir fry for a minute. Serve with brown rice or quinoa.

Chinese Broccoli, Chicken & Cherry Tomatoes Stir Fry
Serves 2

Ingredients - Allergies: SF, GF, DF, EF

- 1/2 pound chicken
- 1 cup sliced Chinese broccoli
- 1 cup halved cherry tomatoes
- 1/4 cup sliced onions
- 1/2 cup cashews
- 1 Tsp. oil

Instructions

Marinade chicken in a Superfoods marinade. Stir fry drained chicken in coconut oil for few minutes, add all vegetables and stir fry for 2 more minutes. Add the rest of the marinade and stir fry for a minute. Serve with brown rice or quinoa.

Baby Squid, Sprouts & Spring Onions Stir Fry

Serves 2

Ingredients - Allergies: SF, GF, DF, EF

- 1/2 pound baby squid
- 1 cup sprouts
- 1/2 cup sliced spring onions
- 1/2 cup sliced red peppers
- 1/4 cup chili sauce (mix chili flakes with oil and salt)
- 1 tsp. minced garlic and ginger each
- 1 Tsp. oil

Instructions

Marinade baby squid in a chili sauce, garlic and ginger. Stir fry drained squid in coconut oil for few minutes, add all vegetables and stir fry for 2 more minutes. Add the rest of the marinade (if any) and stir fry for a minute. Serve with brown rice or quinoa.

Chinese Eggplant, Lotus Root & Chicken Stir Fry

Serves 2

Ingredients - Allergies: SF, GF, DF, EF

- 1/2 pound chicken
- 1 cup sliced Chinese eggplant
- 1/2 cup sliced carrots
- 1/2 cup sliced onions
- 1/2 cup sliced lotus root
- 1 Tsp. oil

Instructions

Marinade chicken and eggplant in a Superfoods marinade. Stir fry drained chicken and eggplant in coconut oil for few minutes, add all vegetables and stir fry for 2 more minutes. Add the rest of the marinade and stir fry for a minute. Serve with brown rice or quinoa.

Green Beans, Chicken Chili Sauce & Onions Stir Fry
Serves 2

Ingredients - Allergies: SF, GF, DF, EF

- 1/2 pound chicken
- 1 cup sliced Green Beans
- 1/2 cup sliced onions
- 1/4 cup chili sauce (mix chili flakes with oil and salt)
- 1 tsp. minced garlic and ginger each
- 1 Tsp. oil

Instructions
Marinade chicken in a chili sauce, ginger and garlic. Stir fry drained chicken in coconut oil for few minutes, add all vegetables and stir fry for 2 more minutes. Add the rest of the marinade and stir fry for a minute. Serve with brown rice or quinoa.

Asparagus, Shrimp & Mushrooms Stir Fry
Serves 2

Ingredients - Allergies: SF, GF, DF, EF

- 1/2 pound shrimp
- 1 cup sliced Asparagus
- 1 cup sliced mushrooms
- 1 Tsp. oil

Instructions

Marinade shrimp in a Superfoods marinade. Stir fry drained shrimp in coconut oil for few minutes, add all vegetables and stir fry for 2 more minutes. Add the rest of the marinade and stir fry for a minute. Serve with brown rice or quinoa.

Edamame, Asparagus, Pork & Snow Peas Stir Fry

Serves 2

Ingredients - Allergies: SF, GF, DF, EF

- 1/2 pound cubed pork
- 1 cup sliced Asparagus
- 1/2 cup snow peas
- 1/2 cup sliced onions
- 1/2 cup edamame
- 1 Tsp. oil

Instructions

Marinade pork in a Superfoods marinade. Stir fry drained pork in coconut oil for few minutes, add all vegetables and stir fry for 2 more minutes. Add the rest of the marinade and stir fry for a minute. Serve with brown rice or quinoa.

Snow Peas, Shrimp & Bok Choy Stir Fry
Serves 2

Ingredients - Allergies: SF, GF, DF, EF

- 1/2 pound shrimp
- 1 cup sliced Green Peas
- 1 cup sliced bok choy
- 1/2 cup sliced onions
- 1 Tsp. oil

Instructions

Marinade shrimp in a Superfoods marinade. Stir fry drained shrimp in coconut oil for few minutes, add all vegetables and stir fry for 2 more minutes. Add the rest of the marinade and stir fry for a minute. Serve with brown rice or quinoa.

Sprouts, Shrimp & Julienned Carrots Stir Fry

Serves 2

Ingredients - Allergies: SF, GF, DF, EF

- 1/2 pound shrimp
- 1 cup Sprouts
- 1/2 cup julienned carrots
- 1/2 cup sliced onions
- 1 Tsp. oil

Instructions

Marinade shrimp in a Superfoods marinade. Stir fry drained shrimp in coconut oil for few minutes, add all vegetables and stir fry for 2 more minutes. Add the rest of the marinade and stir fry for a minute. Serve with brown rice or quinoa.

Water Chestnut, Chicken & Broccoli Stir Fry

Serves 2

Ingredients - Allergies: SF, GF, DF, EF

- 1/2 pound cubed pork
- 1 cup sliced Broccoli
- 1/2 cup sliced celery
- 1/2 cup sliced onions
- 1 cup sliced water chestnuts
- 1 Tsp. oil

Instructions

Marinade pork in a Superfoods marinade. Stir fry drained pork in coconut oil for few minutes, add all vegetables and stir fry for 2 more minutes. Add the rest of the marinade and stir fry for a minute. Serve with brown rice or quinoa.

Asparagus, Red Peppers & Pork Stir Fry

Serves 2

Ingredients - Allergies: SF, GF, DF, EF

- 1/2 pound cubed pork
- 1 cup sliced Asparagus
- 1/2 cup sliced celery
- 1/2 cup sliced onions
- 1 cup sliced Red Peppers
- 1 Tsp. oil

Instructions

Marinade pork in a Superfoods marinade. Stir fry drained pork in coconut oil for few minutes, add all vegetables and stir fry for 2 more minutes. Add the rest of the marinade and stir fry for a minute. Serve with brown rice or quinoa.

Baby Corn, Shrimp, Sprouts & Broccoli Stir Fry

Serves 2

Ingredients - Allergies: SF, GF, DF, EF

- 1/2 pound shrimp
- 1 cup sliced Broccoli
- 1/2 cup julienned carrots
- 1/2 cup sprouts
- 1 cup baby corn
- 1 Tsp. oil

Instructions

Marinade shrimp in a Superfoods marinade. Stir fry drained shrimp in coconut oil for few minutes, add all vegetables and stir fry for 2 more minutes. Add the rest of the marinade and stir fry for a minute. Serve with brown rice or quinoa.

Beef Broth, Asparagus & Onions Stir Fry

Serves 2

Ingredients - Allergies: SF, GF, DF, EF

- 1/2 pound cubed beef
- 2 cups asparagus
- 1/2 cup sliced celery
- 1/2 cup sliced onion
- 1 Tsp. oil

Instructions

Marinade beef in a Superfoods marinade. Stir fry drained beef in coconut oil for few minutes, add all vegetables and stir fry for 2 more minutes. Add the rest of the marinade and stir fry for a minute. Serve with brown rice or quinoa.

Green Beans, Cashews & Pork Stir Fry

Serves 2

Ingredients - Allergies: SF, GF, DF, EF

- 1/2 pound cubed pork
- 1 cup sliced green beans
- 1/2 cup sliced celery
- 1/2 cup sliced onions
- 1/2 cup cashews
- 1 Tsp. oil

Instructions

Marinade pork in a Superfoods marinade. Stir fry drained pork in coconut oil for few minutes, add all vegetables and stir fry for 2 more minutes. Add the rest of the marinade and stir fry for a minute. Serve with brown rice or quinoa.

Pineapple, Red Pepers, Onions & Beef Stir Fry

Serves 2

Ingredients - Allergies: SF, GF, DF, EF

- 1/2 pound cubed beef
- 1 cup sliced pineapple
- 1/2 cup sliced Red peppers
- 1/2 cup sliced onions
- 1/2 cup sliced Green peppers
- 1 Tsp. oil

Instructions

Marinade beef in a Superfoods marinade. Stir fry drained beef in coconut oil for few minutes, add all vegetables and stir fry for 2 more minutes. Add the rest of the marinade and stir fry for a minute. Serve with brown rice or quinoa.

Carrot, Chicken, Onions & Broccoli Stir Fry
Serves 2

Ingredients - Allergies: SF, GF, DF, EF

- 1/2 pound cubed chicken
- 1 cup sliced Broccoli
- 1/2 cup sliced celery
- 1/2 cup sliced green onions
- 1/2 cup sliced carrots
- 1 Tsp. oil

Instructions

Marinade chicken in a Superfoods marinade. Stir fry drained chicken in coconut oil for few minutes, add all vegetables and stir fry for 2 more minutes. Add the rest of the marinade and stir fry for a minute. Serve with brown rice or quinoa.

Eggplant, Green Peppers & Minced Pork Stir Fry

Serves 2

Ingredients - Allergies: SF, GF, DF, EF

- 1/2 pound minced pork
- 2 cups sliced eggplant
- 1/2 cup sliced celery
- 1/2 cup sliced onions
- 1/2 cup sliced carrot
- 1 Tsp. oil

Instructions

Marinade pork in a Superfoods marinade. Stir fry drained pork in coconut oil for few minutes, add all vegetables and stir fry for 2 more minutes. Add the rest of the marinade and stir fry for a minute. Serve with brown rice or quinoa.

Chives, Carrot & Pork Stir Fry
Serves 2

Ingredients - Allergies: SF, GF, DF, EF

- 1/2 pound cubed pork
- 1 + 1/2 cup chives
- 1/2 cup sliced celery
- 1/2 cup sliced onions
- 1/2 cup sliced carrot
- 1 Tsp. oil

Instructions

Marinade pork in a Superfoods marinade. Stir fry drained pork in coconut oil for few minutes, add all vegetables and stir fry for 2 more minutes. Add the rest of the marinade and stir fry for a minute. Serve with brown rice or quinoa.

Green Onions, Ground Cashews & Pork Stir Fry

Serves 2

Ingredients - Allergies: SF, GF, DF, EF

- 1/2 pound cubed pork
- 1 cup sliced Green onions
- 1/2 cup sliced celery
- 1/2 cup sliced Green Peppers
- 1/2 cup ground cashews
- 1 Tsp. oil

Instructions

Marinade pork in a Superfoods marinade. Stir fry drained pork in coconut oil for few minutes, add all vegetables and stir fry for 2 more minutes. Add the rest of the marinade and stir fry for a minute. Serve with brown rice or quinoa.

Asparagus, Shrimp & Sprouts Stir Fry
Serves 2

Ingredients - Allergies: SF, GF, DF, EF

- 1/2 pound shrimp
- 2 cups sliced Asparagus
- 1/2 cup sliced celery
- 1/2 cup sliced onions
- 1 Tsp. coconut oil

Instructions

Marinade shrimp in a Superfoods marinade. Stir fry drained shrimp in coconut oil for few minutes, add all vegetables and stir fry for 2 more minutes. Add the rest of the marinade and stir fry for a minute. Serve with brown rice or quinoa.

Baby Corn, Snow Peas & Chicken Stir Fry

Serves 2

Ingredients - Allergies: SF, GF, DF, EF

- 1/2 pound chicken
- 1 cup baby corn
- 1/2 cup snow peas
- 1/2 cup julienned carrot
- 1/2 cup sliced mushrooms
- 1/2 cup sliced red peppers
- 1 Tsp. coconut oil

Instructions

Marinade shrimp in a Superfoods marinade. Stir fry drained chicken in coconut oil for few minutes, add all vegetables and stir fry for 2 more minutes. Add the rest of the marinade and stir fry for a minute. Serve with brown rice or quinoa.

Bamboo Shoots & Chinese Celery Stir Fry

Serves 2

Ingredients - Allergies: SF, GF, DF, EF

- 3 cups sliced bamboo shoots
- 2 cups sliced Chinese celery
- 1/2 cup sliced onions
- 1 Tsp. coconut oil

Instructions
Stir fry bamboo shoots in coconut oil for few minutes, add Chinese celery and onions and stir fry for 2 more minutes. Add the superfoods marinade and stir fry for a minute. Serve with brown rice or quinoa.

Carrot, Sesame & Spicy Beef Stir Fry

Serves 2

Ingredients - Allergies: SF, GF, DF, EF

- 1/2 pound beef
- 2 cups sliced carrots
- 1/2 cup sesame seeds
- 1/2 cup sliced onions
- 1 Tsp. coconut oil

Instructions

Marinade shrimp in a Superfoods marinade (add 1 Tbsp. ground cumin). Stir fry beef in coconut oil for few minutes, add all vegetables and stir fry for 2 more minutes. Add the rest of the marinade and stir fry for a minute. Sprinkle with sesame seeds and serve with brown rice or quinoa.

Green Pepper, Onion & BlackPeper Beef Stir Fry
Serves 2

Ingredients - Allergies: SF, GF, DF, EF

- 1/2 pound beef stripes
- 1 cup sliced green pepper
- 1/2 cup sliced celery
- 1/2 cup sliced onions
- 1 Tsp. coconut oil
- 1 Tsp. black pepper

Instructions
Marinade beef in a Superfoods marinade (add 1Tbsp. black pepper). Stir fry drained beef in coconut oil for few minutes, add all vegetables and stir fry for 2 more minutes. Add the rest of the marinade and stir fry for a minute. Serve with brown rice or quinoa.

String Beans, Onion & Beef Stir Fry
Serves 2

Ingredients - Allergies: SF, GF, DF, EF

- 1/2 pound beef
- 2 cups sliced string onion
- 1/2 cup sliced onions
- 1 red chili pepper
- 1 Tsp. coconut oil

Instructions
Marinade shrimp in a Superfoods marinade. Stir fry drained shrimp in coconut oil for few minutes, add all vegetables and stir fry for 2 more minutes. Add the rest of the marinade and stir fry for a minute. Serve with brown rice or quinoa.

Cumin Beef & Spinach Stir Fry
Serves 2

Ingredients - Allergies: SF, GF, DF, EF

- 1/2 pound beef
- 1 cup sliced Spinach
- 1 cup sliced Chinese celery
- 1/2 cup sliced onions
- 1 Tsp. coconut oil
- 2 Tsp. ground cumin

Instructions

Marinade beef in a Superfoods marinade (add ground cumin). Stir fry drained beef in coconut oil for few minutes, add onions and Chinese celery and stir fry for 2 more minutes. Add the rest of the marinade and spinach and stir fry for a minute. Serve with brown rice or quinoa.

Bitter Gourd & Minced Meat Stir Fry

Serves 2

Ingredients - Allergies: SF, GF, DF, EF

- 1/2 pound minced beef
- 2 cups sliced bitter gourd
- 1/2 cup sprouts
- 1/2 cup sliced onions
- 1 Tsp. coconut oil

Instructions
Marinade minced beef in a Superfoods marinade. Stir fry drained minced beef in coconut oil for few minutes, add all vegetables and stir fry for 2 more minutes. Add the rest of the marinade and stir fry for a minute. Serve with brown rice or quinoa.

Chicken, Mushrooms & Asparagus Stir Fry
Serves 2

Ingredients - Allergies: SF, GF, DF, EF

- 1/2 pound chicken breast meat
- 1 cups sliced Asparagus
- 1/2 cup sliced carrot
- 1/2 cup sliced mushrooms
- 1 Tsp. coconut oil

Instructions

Marinade chicken in a Superfoods marinade. Stir fry drained chicken in coconut oil for few minutes, add all vegetables and stir fry for 2 more minutes. Add the rest of the marinade and stir fry for a minute. Serve with brown rice or quinoa.

Snow Peas, Chicken & Asparagus Stir Fry

Serves 2

Ingredients - Allergies: SF, GF, DF, EF

- 1/2 pound chicken
- 2 cups sliced snow peas
- 1/2 cup sliced asparagus
- 1/2 cup julienned carrots
- 1 Tsp. coconut oil

Instructions

Marinade chicken in a Superfoods marinade. Stir fry drained chicken in coconut oil for few minutes, add all vegetables and stir fry for 2 more minutes. Add the rest of the marinade and stir fry for a minute. Serve with brown rice or quinoa.

Fish, Sprouts, Chinese Celery & Dill Stir Fry

Serves 2

Ingredients - Allergies: SF, GF, DF, EF

- 1/2 pound fish of your choice
- 2 cups sprouts
- 2 cup sliced Chinese celery
- 1/2 cup sliced dill
- 1 Tsp. coconut oil

Instructions

Marinade fish in a Superfoods marinade. Stir fry drained fish in coconut oil for few minutes, add all vegetables and stir fry for 2 more minutes. Add the rest of the marinade and stir fry for a minute. Serve with brown rice or quinoa.

Beef & Snow Peas Stir Fry

Serves 2

Ingredients - Allergies: SF, GF, DF, EF

- 1/2 pound beef
- 2 cups sliced Snow Peas
- 1/2 of the small onion, sliced
- 1 Tsp. coconut oil
- 1 Tsp. red pepper flakes

Instructions

Marinade beef in a Superfoods marinade (add red pepper flakes). Stir fry drained beef in coconut oil for few minutes, add onions and Snow Peas and stir fry for 2 more minutes. Add the rest of the marinade and stir fry for a minute. Serve with brown rice or quinoa.

Beef & Yellow Peppers Stir Fry
Serves 2

Ingredients - Allergies: SF, GF, DF, EF

- 1/2 pound beef
- 2 sliced Yellow Peppers
- 1 sliced Red or Orange pepper
- 1/2 cup sliced onions
- 1 Tsp. coconut oil
- 1/2 cup broccoli florets
- 1/2 cup mushrooms
- 1/2 cup sliced zucchini or celery or both

Instructions

Marinade beef in a Superfoods marinade. Stir fry drained beef in coconut oil for few minutes, add all veggies and stir fry for 2 more minutes. Add the rest of the marinade and stir fry for a minute. Serve with brown rice or quinoa.

Bok Choy & Seaweed Stir Fry

Serves 2

Ingredients - Allergies: SF, GF, DF, EF

- 2 cups sliced Bok Choy
- 1/2 cup dried mixed seaweed
- 1/2 cup julienned carrots
- 2 tbsp. bonito flakes
- 1 Tsp. coconut oil

Instructions

Put the dried seaweed in lots of water and soak for 10-15 minutes. At the same time marinade sliced bok choy in Superfoods marinade for 15 minutes. Stir fry drained bok choy in coconut oil for 1 minute, add carrots, squeezed out seaweed and the rest of the marinade and stir fry for 1 more minute. Top with bonito flakes. Serve with brown rice or quinoa.

Chicken & Bok Choy Stir Fry
Serves 2

Ingredients - Allergies: SF, GF, DF, EF

- 1/2 pound chicken
- 2 cups sliced Bok Choy
- 1/4 cup sliced Chinese celery
- 1/2 cup sliced onions
- 1 Tsp. coconut oil

Instructions
Marinade chicken in a Superfoods marinade. Stir fry drained chicken in coconut oil for few minutes, add onions and Chinese celery and stir fry for 2 more minutes. Add the rest of the marinade and bok choy and stir fry for a minute. Serve with brown rice or quinoa.

Chicken, Bok Choy, Snow Peas & Peanuts Stir Fry
Serves 2

Ingredients - Allergies: SF, GF, DF, EF

- 1/2 pound chicken
- 1 cup sliced Bok choy
- 1 cup Snow Peas
- 1/2 cup sliced onions
- 1 Tsp. coconut oil
- 2 Tbsp. peanuts

Instructions
Marinade chicken in a Superfoods marinade. Stir fry drained chicken and peanuts in coconut oil for few minutes, add onions, snow peas and bok choy and stir fry for 2 more minutes. Add the rest of the marinade and stir fry for a minute. Serve with brown rice or quinoa.

Mongolian Stir Fry
Serves 2

Ingredients - Allergies: SF, GF, DF, EF

- 1/2 pound beef
- 1 cup sliced zucchini
- 1 cup sliced carrots
- 1/2 cup sliced onions
- 1/2 cup sliced green peppers
- 1 Tsp. coconut oil
- 2 Tsp. ground cumin

Instructions

Marinade beef, carrots and zucchini in a Superfoods marinade (add ground cumin). Stir fry drained beef and veggies in coconut oil for few minutes, add onions and green peppers and stir fry for 2 more minutes. Add the rest of the marinade and stir fry for a minute. Serve with brown rice or quinoa.

Mushrooms, Snow Peas & Bok Choy Stir Fry

Serves 2

Ingredients - Allergies: SF, GF, DF, EF

- 1/2 pound mushrooms
- 1 cup Snow Peas
- 1 cup sliced Bok Choy
- 1/2 cup sliced onions
- 1 Tsp. coconut oil

Instructions

Marinade mushrooms in a Superfoods marinade. Stir fry drained mushrooms in coconut oil for few minutes, add onions and Snow Peas and stir fry for 2 more minutes. Add the rest of the marinade and bok choy and stir fry for a minute. Serve with brown rice or quinoa.

Pork, Red Peppers, Carrots, Celery & Basil Stir Fry
Serves 2

Ingredients - Allergies: SF, GF, DF, EF

- 1/2 pound cubed pork
- 1 cup sliced Red Peppers
- 1/2 cup sliced celery
- 1/2 cup sliced carrots
- 1 Tsp. coconut oil
- 2 Tbsp. sliced Basil leaves

Instructions

Marinade pork in a Superfoods marinade. Stir fry drained pork in coconut oil for few minutes, add carrots and celery and stir fry for 2 more minutes. Add the rest of the marinade and basil leaves and stir fry for a minute. Serve with brown rice or quinoa.

Pork, Zucchini & Onions Stir Fry

Serves 2

Ingredients - Allergies: SF, GF, DF, EF

- 1/2 pound pork
- 1 cup sliced Zucchini
- 1 cup sliced onions
- 1 Tsp. coconut oil

Instructions

Marinade pork in a Superfoods marinade. Stir fry drained pork in coconut oil for few minutes, add zucchini and onions and stir fry for 2 more minutes. Add the rest of the marinade and stir fry for a minute. Serve with brown rice or quinoa.

Snow Peas, Shrimp, Mushrooms & Bok Choy Stir Fry

Serves 2

Ingredients - Allergies: SF, GF, DF, EF

- 1/2 pound shrimp
- 1 cup sliced Snow peas
- 1 cup sliced Chinese celery
- 1/2 cup sliced mushrooms
- 1 Tsp. coconut oil

Instructions

Marinade shrimp in a Superfoods marinade. Stir fry drained shrimp in coconut oil for few minutes, add snow peas and Chinese celery and stir fry for 2 more minutes. Add the rest of the marinade and mushrooms and stir fry for a minute. Serve with brown rice or quinoa.

Eggplant, Red Peppers & Carrots Stir Fry

Serves 2

Ingredients - Allergies: SF, GF, DF, EF

- 1/2 pound Red Peppers
- 1 + 1/2 cup sliced Eggplant
- 1 cup sliced Carrots
- 1/2 cup sliced onions
- 1 Tsp. coconut oil

Instructions

Marinade eggplant in a Superfoods marinade. Stir fry drained eggplant and carrots in coconut oil for 5 minutes, add red peppers and onions, stir fry for 2 more minutes. Add the rest of the marinade and stir fry for a minute. Serve with brown rice or quinoa.

Eggplant, Shiitake & Bamboo Shoots Stir Fry

Serves 2

Ingredients - Allergies: SF, GF, DF, EF

- 1/2 pound sliced shiitake mushrooms
- 1 cup sliced eggplant
- 1 cup sliced Green peppers
- 1/2 cup sliced carrots
- 1/2 cup sliced onions
- 1/2 cup sliced bamboo shoots
- 1 Tsp. coconut oil

Instructions

Marinade shiitake, bamboo shoots and eggplant in a Superfoods marinade. Stir fry drained eggplant and bamboo shoots in coconut oil for 5 minutes, add carrots and onions and stir fry for 2 more minutes. Add the rest of the marinade with shiitake and stir fry for a minute. Serve with brown rice or quinoa.

Korean Squid Stir Fry

Serves 2

Ingredients - Allergies: SF, GF, DF, EF

- 1 pound Squid stripes
- 1 cup sliced carrots
- 1/2 cup Korean Spicy marinade
- 1/2 cup sliced onions
- 1 Tsp. coconut oil

Instructions
Marinade squid stripes in a Korean spicy marinade. Stir fry drained squid in coconut oil for few minutes, add carrots and onions and stir fry for 2 more minutes. Add the rest of the marinade and stir fry for a minute. Serve with brown rice or quinoa.

Okra, Sprouts & Onions Choy Stir Fry
Serves 2

Ingredients - Allergies: SF, GF, DF, EF

- 1 + 1/2 pound sliced okra
- 1 cup sprouts
- 1/2 cup sliced onions
- 1 Tsp. coconut oil

Instructions

Marinade okra in a Superfoods marinade. Stir fry drained okra in coconut oil for few minutes, add onions and stir fry for 2 more minutes. Add the rest of the marinade and sprouts and stir fry for a minute. Serve with brown rice or quinoa.

Okra, Asparagus, Chicken & Onions Stir Fry
Serves 2

Ingredients - Allergies: SF, GF, DF, EF

- 1/2 pound chicken
- 1 cup sliced okra
- 1 cup sliced asparagus
- 1/2 cup sliced onions
- 1 Tsp. coconut oil

Instructions
Marinade chicken in a Korean Spicy marinade. Stir fry drained chicken in coconut oil for few minutes, add okra and asparagus and stir fry for 2 more minutes. Add the rest of the marinade and onions and stir fry for a minute. Serve with brown rice or quinoa.

Okra, Ground Beef, Red Peppers & Cilantro Stir Fry
Serves 2

Ingredients - Allergies: SF, GF, DF, EF

- 1/2 pound ground beef
- 1 cup sliced okra
- 1 cup sliced red peppers
- 1/2 cup sliced onions
- 1/4 cup sliced cilantro
- 1 Tsp. coconut oil

Instructions
Marinade okra in a Superfoods marinade. Stir fry drained okra and ground beef in coconut oil for few minutes, add red peppers and onions and stir fry for 2 more minutes. Add the rest of the marinade and half of cilantro and stir fry for a minute. Decorate with the rest of cilantro. Serve with brown rice or quinoa.

Pork, Broccoli, Baby Carrots & Mushrooms Stir Fry

Serves 2

Ingredients - Allergies: SF, GF, DF, EF

- 1/2 pound cubed pork
- 1 cup sliced Broccoli
- 1 cup halved lengthwise baby carrots
- 1/2 cup sliced mushrooms
- 1 Tsp. coconut oil

Instructions

Marinade pork in a Superfoods marinade. Stir fry drained pork in coconut oil for few minutes, add broccoli and baby carrots and stir fry for 2 more minutes. Add the rest of the marinade and mushrooms and stir fry for a minute. Serve with brown rice or quinoa.

Pork, Red Peppers, Broccoli & Carrots Stir Fry
Serves 2

Ingredients - Allergies: SF, GF, DF, EF

- 1/2 pound pork
- 1 cup sliced Red Peppers
- 1 cup sliced Broccoli
- 1/2 cup sliced carrots
- 1 Tsp. coconut oil

Instructions

Marinade pork in a Superfoods marinade. Stir fry drained pork in coconut oil for few minutes, add broccoli and carrots and stir fry for 2 more minutes. Add the rest of the marinade and red peppers and stir fry for a minute. Serve with brown rice or quinoa.

Green Peas, Pork, Onions & Cilntro Stir Fry
Serves 2

Ingredients - Allergies: SF, GF, DF, EF

- 1/2 pound pork
- 1 cup Green peas
- 1 cup sliced onions
- 1/4 cup cilantro
- 1 Tsp. coconut oil

Instructions
Marinade pork in a Superfoods marinade. Stir fry drained pork and green peas in coconut oil for few minutes, add onions and stir fry for 2 more minutes. Add the rest of the marinade and stir fry for a minute. Serve with brown rice or quinoa.

Bitter Gourd, Shrimp & Squid Stir Fry
Serves 2

Ingredients - Allergies: SF, GF, DF, EF

- 1/2 pound squid slices
- 1/2 pound shrimp
- 1 cup sliced bitter gourd
- 1/2 cup sliced onions
- 1 Tsp. coconut oil

Instructions
Marinade shrimp and squid in a Superfoods marinade. Stir fry drained shrimp and squid in coconut oil for few minutes, add bitter gourd and stir fry for 2 more minutes. Add the rest of the marinade and onions and stir fry for a minute. Serve with brown rice or quinoa.

Baby Carrots & Shrimp Stir Fry

Serves 2

Ingredients - Allergies: SF, GF, DF, EF

- 1/2 pound shrimp
- 1 cup baby carrots
- 1/2 cup sliced Broccoli
- 1/2 cup sliced mushrooms
- 1 Tsp. coconut oil

Instructions

Marinade pork in a Superfoods marinade. Stir fry drained shrimp in coconut oil for few minutes, add broccoli and carrots and stir fry for 2 more minutes. Add the rest of the marinade and mushrooms and stir fry for a minute. Serve with brown rice or quinoa.

Beef, Onions & Chili Stir Fry
Serves 2

Ingredients - Allergies: SF, GF, DF, EF

- 1/2 pound beef
- 1 cup sliced onions
- 1/2 cup sliced celery
- 1 Tsp. coconut oil
- 1 Tsp. chili sauce (to taste)

Instructions
Marinade pork in a Superfoods marinade with chili sauce added. Stir fry drained beef in coconut oil for few minutes, add onions and celery and stir fry for 2 more minutes. Add the rest of the marinade and red peppers and stir fry for a minute. Serve with brown rice or quinoa.

Black Pepper Beef & Green Peppers Stir Fry
Serves 2

Ingredients - Allergies: SF, GF, DF, EF

- 1/2 pound beef
- 1 cup sliced Green Peppers
- 1 cup sliced Onion
- 1/2 cup sliced celery
- 1 Tsp. coconut oil

Instructions
Marinade beef in a Superfoods marinade. Stir fry drained beef in coconut oil for few minutes, add celery and onions and stir fry for 2 more minutes. Add the rest of the marinade and green peppers and stir fry for a minute. Serve with brown rice or quinoa.

Lamb, Mushrooms & Broccoli Stir Fry
Serves 2

Ingredients - Allergies: SF, GF, DF, EF
- 1/2 pound lamb
- 1 cup sliced Mushrooms
- 1 cup sliced Broccoli
- 1/2 cup sliced onions
- 1 Tsp. coconut oil

Instructions
Marinade lamb in a Superfoods marinade. Stir fry drained lamb in coconut oil for few minutes, add broccoli and onions and stir fry for 2 more minutes. Add the rest of the marinade and mushrooms and stir fry for a minute. Serve with brown rice or quinoa.

Pork, Carrots & Spinach Stir Fry

Serves 2

Ingredients - Allergies: SF, GF, DF, EF

- 1/2 pound pork
- 1 cup spinach
- 1 cup sliced carrots
- 1 Tsp. coconut oil

Instructions

Marinade pork in a Superfoods marinade. Stir fry drained pork in coconut oil for few minutes, add carrots and stir fry for 2 more minutes. Add the rest of the marinade and spinach and stir fry for a minute. Serve with brown rice or quinoa.

Pork, Bok Choy & GreenPeppers Stir Fry
Serves 2

Ingredients - Allergies: SF, GF, DF, EF

- 1/2 pound pork
- 1 cup sliced Green Peppers
- 1 cup sliced Bok Choy
- 1/2 cup sliced green onions
- 1 Tsp. coconut oil

Instructions

Marinade pork in a Superfoods marinade. Stir fry drained pork in coconut oil for few minutes, add white parts of bok choy and green onions and stir fry for 2 more minutes. Add the rest of the marinade and green peppers and the rest of bok choy and stir fry for a minute. Serve with brown rice or quinoa.

Pork, Green Onions & Red Peppers Stir Fry

Serves 2

Ingredients - Allergies: SF, GF, DF, EF

- 1/2 pound pork
- 1 cup sliced Red Peppers
- 1 cup sliced green onions
- 1/2 cup sliced carrots
- 1 Tsp. coconut oil

Instructions

Marinade pork in a Superfoods marinade. Stir fry drained pork in coconut oil for few minutes, add green onions and carrots and stir fry for 2 more minutes. Add the rest of the marinade and red peppers and stir fry for a minute. Serve with brown rice or quinoa.

Squid, Chinese Cabbage, Green Onions, Zucchini & Chili Pepper Paste Stir Fry

Serves 2

Ingredients - Allergies: SF, GF, DF, EF

- 1/2 pound squid
- 1 cup sliced Chinese cabbage
- 1 cup sliced Zucchini
- 1/2 cup sliced green onions
- 1 Tsp. chili paste (to taste)
- 1 Tsp. coconut oil

Instructions

Marinade squid in a Superfoods marinade with chili sauce. Stir fry drained squid in coconut oil for few minutes, add green onions and zucchini and stir fry for 2 more minutes. Add the rest of the marinade and Chinese cabbage and stir fry for a minute. Serve with brown rice or quinoa.

Water Chectnut, Shrimp & Broccoli Stir Fry

Serves 2

Ingredients - Allergies: SF, GF, DF, EF

- 1/2 pound shrimp
- 1 cup sliced Broccoli
- 1/2 cup sliced water chestnuts
- 1 Tsp. coconut oil

Instructions

Marinade shrimp in a Superfoods marinade. Stir fry drained shrimp in coconut oil for few minutes, add broccoli and water chestnuts and stir fry for 2 more minutes. Add the rest of the marinade and stir fry for a minute. Serve with brown rice or quinoa.

Zucchini, Peppers, Carrots, Mushrooms & Green Beans Stir Fry

Serves 2

Ingredients - Allergies: SF, GF, DF, EF

- 1/2 cup sliced mushrooms
- 1/2 cup sliced Red Peppers
- 1/2 cup sliced Zucchini
- 1/2 cup sliced carrots
- 1/2 cup sliced green beans
- 1/2 cup sliced green onions
- 1 Tsp. coconut oil

Instructions

Marinade zucchini in a Superfoods marinade. Stir fry drained zucchini in coconut oil for few minutes, add all other veggies and stir fry for 4 more minutes. Add the rest of the marinade and stir fry for a minute. Serve with brown rice or quinoa.

Beef, Shitake, Brocoli & Red PeppersStir Fry
Serves 2

Ingredients - Allergies: SF, GF, DF, EF

- 1/2 pound beef
- 1/2 cup sliced Broccoli
- 1/2 cup halved shiitake
- 1/2 cup sliced red peppers
- 1 Tsp. coconut oil

Instructions
Marinade shrimp in a Superfoods marinade. Stir fry drained beef in coconut oil for few minutes, add all veggies and stir fry for 2 more minutes. Add the rest of the marinade and stir fry for a minute. Serve with brown rice or quinoa.

Bok Choy, Celery & Onions Stir Fry
Serves 2

Ingredients - Allergies: SF, GF, DF, EF

- 1/2 pound Bok Choy, sliced
- 1 cup sliced Celery
- 1/2 cup chopped onions
- 1 Tsp. coconut oil

Instructions
Marinade white part of bok choy in a Superfoods marinade. Stir fry drained bok choy in coconut oil for 2 minutes, add celery and onions and stir fry for 2 more minutes. Add sliced green parts of bok choy and the rest of the marinade and stir fry for a minute. Serve with brown rice or quinoa.

Chicken, Green Beans & Snow Peas Stir Fry

Serves 2

Ingredients - Allergies: SF, GF, DF, EF

- 1/2 pound chicken
- 1 cup sliced green beans
- 1/2 cup sliced snow peas
- 1 Tsp. coconut oil

Instructions

Marinade chicken in a Superfoods marinade. Stir fry drained chicken in coconut oil for few minutes, add green beans and snow peas and stir fry for 2 more minutes. Add the rest of the marinade and stir fry for a minute. Serve with brown rice or quinoa.

Mushrooms, Snow Peas & Broccoli Stir Fry

Serves 2

Ingredients - Allergies: SF, GF, DF, EF

- 1/2 pound mushrooms
- 1 cup sliced Broccoli
- 1/2 cup sliced snow peas
- 1 Tsp. coconut oil

Instructions

Marinade mushrooms in a Superfoods marinade. Stir fry drained mushrooms in coconut oil for few minutes, add broccoli and snow peas and stir fry for 2 more minutes. Add the rest of the marinade and stir fry for a minute. Serve with brown rice or quinoa.

Yellow Squash, Zucchini, Eggplant & Onions Stir Fry

Serves 2

Ingredients - Allergies: SF, GF, DF, EF

- 1/4 pound zucchini
- 1/4 pound yellow squash
- 1 cup sliced eggplant
- 1/2 cup sliced onions
- 1 Tsp. coconut oil

Instructions

Marinade eggplant, squash and zucchini in a Superfoods marinade. Stir fry drained veggies in coconut oil for few minutes, add onions and stir fry for 2 more minutes. Add the rest of the marinade and stir fry for a minute. Serve with brown rice or quinoa.

Shiitake, GreenPeppers & Bamboo Shoots Stir Fry
Serves 2

Ingredients - Allergies: SF, GF, DF, EF

- 1/2 pound shiitake
- 1/2 cup sliced black mushrooms
- 1/2 cup sliced green peppers
- 1/2 cup sliced dried bamboo shoots
- 1 Tsp. coconut oil

Instructions
Marinade shiitake in a Superfoods marinade. Stir fry drained shiitake in coconut oil for few minutes, add broccoli and water chestnuts and stir fry for 2 more minutes. Add the rest of the marinade and stir fry for a minute. Serve with brown rice or quinoa.

Shiitake, Shrimp & Asparagus Stir Fry

Serves 2

Ingredients - Allergies: SF, GF, DF, EF

- 1/2 pound shrimp
- 1 cup sliced Asparagus
- 1/2 cup sliced shiitake
- 1 Tsp. coconut oil

Instructions

Marinade shrimp in a Superfoods marinade. Stir fry drained shrimp in coconut oil for few minutes, add asparagus and shiitake and stir fry for 2 more minutes. Add the rest of the marinade and stir fry for a minute. Serve with brown rice or quinoa.

Shrimp, Celery & Garlic Stir Fry
Serves 2

Ingredients - Allergies: SF, GF, DF, EF

- 1/2 pound shrimp
- 1 + 1/2 cup sliced Celery
- 2 minced garlic cloves
- 1 Tsp. coconut oil

Instructions

Marinade shrimp in a Superfoods marinade. Stir fry drained shrimp in coconut oil for few minutes, add celery and garlic and stir fry for 2 more minutes. Add the rest of the marinade and stir fry for a minute. Serve with brown rice or quinoa.

Squid, Shrimp, Celery & Bitter Gourd Stir Fry
Serves 2

Ingredients - Allergies: SF, GF, DF, EF

- 1/4 pound shrimp
- 1/4 pound squid
- 1 cup sliced Celery
- 1/2 cup sliced bitter gourd
- 1 Tsp. coconut oil

Instructions
Marinade shrimp and squid in a Superfoods marinade. Stir fry drained shrimp and squid in coconut oil for few minutes, add celery and biter gourd and stir fry for 2 more minutes. Add the rest of the marinade and stir fry for a minute. Serve with brown rice or quinoa.

Sechuan Beef, Celery, Carrot & Chili Sauce Stir Fry
Serves 2

Ingredients - Allergies: SF, GF, DF, EF

- 1/2 pound beef
- 1 cup sliced celery
- 1/2 cup sliced carrot
- 1 Tsp. coconut oil

Instructions
Marinade beef in a Superfoods marinade and chili sauce. Stir fry drained beef in coconut oil for few minutes, add celery and carrot and stir fry for 2 more minutes. Add the rest of the marinade and stir fry for a minute. Serve with brown rice or quinoa.

Asparagus, Yellow Peppers & Tomato Stir Fry

Serves 2

Ingredients - Allergies: SF, GF, DF, EF

- 1/2 pound asparagus
- 1 cup sliced Yellow peppers
- 1 cup chopped tomato
- 1 Tsp. coconut oil

Instructions

Marinade asparagus in a Superfoods marinade. Stir fry drained asparagus in coconut oil for 7-8 minutes, add peppers and tomato and stir fry for 2 more minutes. Add the rest of the marinade and stir fry for a minute. Serve with brown rice or quinoa.

Beef, Sprouts, Yellow Peppers & Snow Peas Stir Fry
Serves 2

Ingredients - Allergies: SF, GF, DF, EF

- 1/2 pound beef
- 1 cup sprouts
- 1 cup Yellow peppers
- 1/2 cup snow peas
- 1 Tsp. coconut oil

Instructions
Marinade beef in a Superfoods marinade. Stir fry drained beef in coconut oil for few minutes, add yellow peppers and snow peas and stir fry for 2 more minutes. Add sprouts and the rest of the marinade and stir fry for a minute. Serve with brown rice or quinoa.

Bok Choy, Almonds, Onions & Sesame Stir Fry
Serves 2

Ingredients - Allergies: SF, GF, DF, EF

- 1/2 pound bok choy
- 1 + ½ cup sliced onions
- 3 Tbsp. almond slices
- 1 Tbsp. sesame seeds
- 1 Tsp. coconut oil

Instructions

Marinade bok choy in a Superfoods marinade. Stir fry drained bok choy and onions in coconut oil for few minutes, add almond and sesame seeds and stir fry for 2 more minutes. Add the rest of the marinade and stir fry for a minute. Serve with brown rice or quinoa.

Broccoli, Turkey Breast & Carrots Stir Fry
Serves 2

Ingredients - Allergies: SF, GF, DF, EF

- 1/2 pound turkey breast, cubed
- 1 cup sliced broccoli
- 3/4 cup sliced carrots
- 1 Tsp. coconut oil

Instructions

Marinade turkey in a Superfoods marinade. Stir fry drained turkey in coconut oil for few minutes, add carrot and broccoli and stir fry for 2 more minutes. Add the rest of the marinade and stir fry for a minute. Serve with brown rice or quinoa.

Broccolini, Zucchini, Tomatoes & Onions Stir Fry
Serves 2

Ingredients - Allergies: SF, GF, DF, EF

- 1/2 pound broccolini
- 1 cup sliced zucchini
- 3/4 cup sliced onions
- 3/4 cup chopped tomato
- 1 Tsp. coconut oil

Instructions
Marinade broccolini in a Superfoods marinade. Stir fry drained broccolini in coconut oil for few minutes, add zucchini and onions and stir fry for 2 more minutes. Add tomatoes and the rest of the marinade and stir fry for a minute. Serve with brown rice or quinoa.

Chicken, Green Beans & Snow Peas Stir Fry
Serves 2

Ingredients - Allergies: SF, GF, DF, EF

- 1/2 pound chicken
- 1 cup halved asparagus
- 1 cup snow peas
- 1 Tbsp. sliced green onions
- 1 Tsp. coconut oil

Instructions
Marinade chicken in a Superfoods marinade. Stir fry drained chicken and asparagus in coconut oil for few minutes, add snow peas and stir fry for 4-5 more minutes. Add the rest of the marinade and stir fry for a minute. Sprinkle with green onions. Serve with brown rice or quinoa.

Eggplant, Mushrooms, Carrots & Snow Peas Stir Fry

Serves 2

Ingredients - Allergies: SF, GF, DF, EF

- 1/2 pound eggplant
- 1 + 1/2 cup mushrooms
- 1/2 cup sliced carrot
- 1 cup sliced snow peas
- 1 minced garlic clove
- 1 Tsp. coconut oil

Instructions

Marinade eggplant in a Superfoods marinade. Stir fry drained eggplant in coconut oil for few minutes, add carrot, snow peas and garlic and stir fry for 2 more minutes. Add the rest of the marinade and stir fry for a minute. Serve with brown rice or quinoa.

Kale, Baby Corn & Shrimp Stir Fry
Serves 2

Ingredients - Allergies: SF, GF, DF, EF

- 1/2 pound shrimp
- 1 + 1/2 cup sliced Kale
- 1 cup baby corn
- 1 Tsp. coconut oil

Instructions
Marinade shrimp in a Superfoods marinade. Stir fry drained shrimp in coconut oil for few minutes, add kale and baby corn and stir fry for 2 more minutes. Add the rest of the marinade and stir fry for a minute. Serve with brown rice or quinoa.

Lamb, Baby Corn, Red Peppers & Green Beans Stir Fry
Serves 2

Ingredients - Allergies: SF, GF, DF, EF

- 1/2 pound lamb
- 1 cup sliced red peppers
- 3/4 cup sliced green beans
- 1/2 cup baby corn
- 1 Tsp. coconut oil

Instructions
Marinade lamb in a Superfoods marinade. Stir fry drained lamb in coconut oil for few minutes, add green beans, baby corn and peppers and stir fry for 2 more minutes. Add the rest of the marinade and stir fry for a minute. Serve with brown rice or quinoa.

Minced Pork, Mushrooms & Red Peppers Stir Fry
Serves 2

Ingredients - Allergies: SF, GF, DF, EF

- 1/2 pound minced pork meat
- 1 + 1/2 cup sliced Mushrooms
- 3/4 cup sliced red peppers
- 3/4 cup sliced green peppers
- 1 Tsp. coconut oil

Instructions
Stir fry minced pork meat in coconut oil for few minutes, add red and green peppers and mushrooms and stir fry for 2 more minutes. Add the superfoods marinade and stir fry for a minute. Serve with brown rice or quinoa.

Brussel Sprouts, Broccoli, Chicken & Leeks Stir Fry

Serves 2

Ingredients - Allergies: SF, GF, DF, EF

- 1/2 pound chicken
- 1 cup sliced Brussels sprouts
- 1 cup broccoli
- 1/2 cup sliced leeks
- 1 Tsp. coconut oil

Instructions
Marinade chicken in a Superfoods marinade. Stir fry drained chicken and Brussels sprouts in coconut oil for few minutes, add leeks and broccoli and stir fry for 4-5 more minutes. Add the rest of the marinade and stir fry for a minute. Serve with brown rice or quinoa.

Chicken, Cashews & Green Beans Stir Fry
Serves 2

Ingredients - Allergies: SF, GF, DF, EF

- 1/2 pound chicken
- 1 cup Green beans
- 1 cup cashews
- 1 Tsp. coconut oil

Instructions

Marinade chicken in a Superfoods marinade. Stir fry drained chicken and green beans in coconut oil for few minutes, add cashews and stir fry for 4-5 more minutes. Add the rest of the marinade and stir fry for a minute. Serve with brown rice or quinoa.

Lamb, Shallots, Red Peppers & Green Onions Stir Fry

Serves 2

Ingredients - Allergies: SF, GF, DF, EF

- 1/2 pound lamb
- 1/2 cup green peppers
- 1 cup red peppers
- 1/2 cup shallots
- 2 Tbsp. sliced green onions
- 1 Tsp. coconut oil

Instructions

Marinade lamb in a Superfoods marinade. Stir fry drained lamb in coconut oil for few minutes, add shallots, green peppers and red peppers and stir fry for 4-5 more minutes. Add the rest of the marinade and stir fry for a minute. Sprinkle with green onions. Serve with brown rice or quinoa.

Mixed Seafood, Green Beans & Sprouts Stir Fry
Serves 2

Ingredients - Allergies: SF, GF, DF, EF

- 1/2 pound mixed seafood
- 1 cup green beans
- 1 cup sprouts
- 1 half of the carrot, sliced
- 1 Tsp. coconut oil

Instructions
Marinade seafood in a Superfoods marinade. Stir fry drained seafood and green beans in coconut oil for few minutes, add carrot and stir fry for 4-5 more minutes. Add the rest of the marinade and sprouts and stir fry for a minute. Serve with brown rice or quinoa.

Pork, Mushrooms & Green Beans Stir Fry

Serves 2

Ingredients - Allergies: SF, GF, DF, EF

- 1/2 pound pork
- 1/2 cup red peppers
- 1 cup green beans
- 1 cup mushrooms
- 1 Tsp. coconut oil

Instructions
Marinade pork in a Superfoods marinade. Stir fry drained pork and green beans in coconut oil for few minutes, add red peppers and mushrooms and stir fry for 4-5 more minutes. Add the rest of the marinade and stir fry for a minute. Serve with brown rice or quinoa.

Prawns & Snow Peas Stir Fry
Serves 2

Ingredients - Allergies: SF, GF, DF, EF

- 1/2 pound prawns
- 2 cups snow peas
- 1 Tbsp. sliced green onions
- 1 Tsp. coconut oil

Instructions

Marinade prawns in a Superfoods marinade. Stir fry drained prawns in coconut oil for few minutes, add snow peas and stir fry for 4-5 more minutes. Add the rest of the marinade and stir fry for a minute. Sprinkle with green onions. Serve with brown rice or quinoa.

Red Peppers, Yellow Peppers & Olives Stir Fry

Serves 2

Ingredients - Allergies: SF, GF, DF, EF

- 1 cup red peppers
- 1 cup green peppers
- 1 cup yellow peppers
- 1/2 cup carrot
- 1 rosemary sprig
- 1 Tbsp. basil leaves
- 1/2 cup olives
- 1 Tsp. coconut oil

Instructions

Marinade all 3 types of peppers in a Superfoods marinade. Stir fry drained peppers and carrot in coconut oil for few minutes, add olives and rosemary and stir fry for 4-5 more minutes. Add the rest of the marinade and basil stir fry for a minute. Serve with brown rice or quinoa.

Spinach, Prawns & Water Chestnut Stir Fry
Serves 2

Ingredients - Allergies: SF, GF, DF, EF

- 1/2 pound prawns
- 1 cup sliced water chestnut
- 1 cup spinach
- 1 Tsp. coconut oil

Instructions

Marinade prawns in a Superfoods marinade. Stir fry drained prawns and water chestnut in coconut oil for 4-5 more minutes. Add the rest of the marinade, spinach and stir fry for a minute. Serve with brown rice or quinoa.

Squid, Shrimp, Mussels & Green Beans Stir Fry
Serves 2

Ingredients - Allergies: SF, GF, DF, EF

- 1/2 pound Squid, shrimp and mussels each
- 1 cup green beans
- 1/2 cup carrots
- 2 Tbsp. basil leaves
- 1 Tsp. coconut oil

Instructions

Marinade squid, shrimp and mussels in a Superfoods marinade. Stir fry drained squid, shrimp and mussels and green beans in coconut oil for few minutes, add carrot and stir fry for 4-5 more minutes. Add the rest of the marinade and stir fry for a minute. Sprinkle with basil leaves and mix. Serve with brown rice or quinoa.

Water Chestnut, Chicken & Bok Choy Stir Fry
Serves 2

Ingredients - Allergies: SF, GF, DF, EF

- 1/2 pound chicken
- 1 cup sliced water chestnuts
- 1 cup sliced carrot
- 1/2 cup sliced bok choy
- 1 Tsp. coconut oil

Instructions

Marinade chicken in a Superfoods marinade. Stir fry drained chicken and water chestnut in coconut oil for few minutes, add carrot and stir fry for 4-5 more minutes. Add the rest of the marinade and stir fry for a minute. Sprinkle with green onions. Serve with brown rice or quinoa.

Baby Corn, Bok Choy, Onion & Beef Stir Fry
Serves 2

Ingredients - Allergies: SF, GF, DF, EF

- 1/2 pound beef stripes
- 1 cup sliced bok choy
- 1/2 cup baby corn
- 1/2 cup onions
- 1 Tsp. coconut oil

Instructions
Marinade beef in a Superfoods marinade. Stir fry drained beef and baby corn in coconut oil for 4-5 more minutes. Add the rest of the marinade, onion and bok choy and stir fry for a minute. Serve with brown rice or quinoa.

Bok Choy, Chicken, Snow Peas & Mushrooms Stir Fry
Serves 2

Ingredients - Allergies: SF, GF, DF, EF

- 1/2 pound chicken
- 1 cup sliced bok choy
- 1/2 cup snow peas
- 1/2 cup mushrooms
- 1 Tsp. coconut oil

Instructions

Marinade chicken in a Superfoods marinade. Stir fry drained chicken and snow peas in coconut oil for 4-5 more minutes. Add the rest of the marinade, mushrooms and stir fry for a minute. Serve with brown rice or quinoa.

Broccoli, Green Onions & Red Peppers Stir Fry
Serves 2

Ingredients - Allergies: SF, GF, DF, EF

- 1/2 pound broccoli, with stalks peeled
- 1 cup red peppers
- 1 cup green onions
- 1 Tsp. coconut oil

Instructions
Marinade peeled and sliced broccoli stalks in a Superfoods marinade.
Stir fry drained broccoli stalks, broccoli florets and red peppers in
coconut oil for 4-5 more minutes. Add the rest of the marinade, green
onions and stir fry for a minute. Serve with brown rice or quinoa.

Leeks & Pork Fry
Serves 2

Ingredients - Allergies: SF, GF, DF, EF

- 1/2 pound pork
- 2 cups diagonally sliced leeks
- 1/2 cup celery
- 1 Tsp. coconut oil

Instructions

Marinade pork in a Superfoods marinade. Stir fry drained pork and leeks in coconut oil for 4-5 more minutes. Add the rest of the marinade, celery and stir fry for a minute. Serve with brown rice or quinoa.

Fennel, Bok Choy, Red Pepper & Celery Stir Fry
Serves 2

Ingredients - Allergies: SF, GF, DF, EF

- 1 cup sliced celery
- 1 cup sliced fennel bulb
- 1/2 cup sliced red peppers
- 1 cup sliced bok choy
- 1 Tsp. coconut oil

Instructions
Marinade fennel in a Superfoods marinade. Stir fry drained fennel and celery in coconut oil for 4-5 more minutes. Add the rest of the marinade, bok choy and red peppers and stir fry for a minute. Serve with brown rice or quinoa.

Fish, Wood Ear Mushrooms & Green Peas Stir Fry
Serves 2

Ingredients - Allergies: SF, GF, DF, EF

- 1/2 pound fish filets (e.g. tilapia, cod, sole, flounder)
- 1 cup wood ear mushrooms, soaked in water for 30 minutes
- 1/2 cup green peas
- 1 Tsp. coconut oil

Instructions
Marinade fish in a Superfoods marinade. Stir fry drained fish and green peas in coconut oil for 4-5 more minutes. Add the rest of the marinade, mushrooms and stir fry for a minute. Serve with brown rice or quinoa.

Fish, Bok Choy, Onions & Tomato Stir Fry
Serves 2

Ingredients - Allergies: SF, GF, DF, EF

- 1/2 pound fish filets (e.g. tilapia, cod, sole, flounder)
- 1 cup sliced bok choy
- 1/2 cup tomato
- 1/2 cup onions
- 1 Tsp. coconut oil

Instructions
Marinade fish in a Superfoods marinade. Stir fry drained fish and onions in coconut oil for 4-5 more minutes. Add the rest of the marinade, bok choy and tomato and stir fry for a minute. Serve with brown rice or quinoa.

Green Garlic, Pork, Ginger & Celery Stir Fry
Serves 2

Ingredients - Allergies: SF, GF, DF, EF

- 1/2 pound pork
- 1 cup sliced green garlic
- 1 Tbsp. minced ginger
- 1 cup celery
- 1 Tsp. coconut oil

Instructions

Marinade pork in a Superfoods marinade. Stir fry drained pork and green garlic in coconut oil for 4-5 more minutes. Add the rest of the marinade, ginger and celery and stir fry for a minute. Serve with brown rice or quinoa.

Kale, Beef, Bok Choy & Green Garlic Stir Fry

Serves 2

Ingredients - Allergies: SF, GF, DF, EF

- 1/2 pound beef
- 1 cup sliced bok choy
- 1 cup sliced kale
- 1/2 cup sliced green garlic
- 1 Tsp. coconut oil

Instructions

Marinade beef in a Superfoods marinade. Stir fry drained beef, green garlic and kale in coconut oil for 4-5 more minutes. Add the rest of the marinade, bok choy and stir fry for a minute. Serve with brown rice or quinoa.

Lamb, Broccoli, Mushrooms & Onions Stir Fry
Serves 2

Ingredients - Allergies: SF, GF, DF, EF

- 1/2 pound lamb
- 1 cup broccoli
- 1 cup mushrooms
- 1/2 cup onions
- 1 Tsp. coconut oil

Instructions

Marinade lamb in a Superfoods marinade. Stir fry drained lamb and broccoli in coconut oil for 4-5 more minutes. Add the rest of the marinade, onions and mushrooms and stir fry for a minute. Serve with brown rice or quinoa.

Bonus Chapter – Superfoods Salads

Figs, Arugula, Walnut & Cheese Salad
Serves 2

Ingredients - Allergies: SF, GF, EF

- 1 cup quartered figs
- 1/2 cup walnuts
- 1/2 cup cheese
- 1 cup arugula

Dressing:
- 1 tbsp. oil
- 1 tbsp. fresh lemon juice
- pinch of black pepper
- pinch of sea salt
- a pinch of oregano

Instructions: Mix all ingredients.

Quinoa & Green Peas Salad

Serves: 6

Ingredients - Allergies: SF, GF, EF

For the salad
- 2 cups cooked
- 2-3 cups frozen green peas
- 1/2 cup low-fat feta cheese
- 6oz.pork, cubed
- 1/2 cup freshly chopped basil and cilantro
- 1/2 cup almonds, pulsed in a food processor until crushed

For the dressing
- 1/3 cup lemon juice (1-2 large juicy lemons)
- 1/3 cup oil
- 1/4 tsp. salt (more to taste)
- a few teaspoons raw honey , to taste

Instructions

Bring a pot of water to boil and then turn off the heat. Add the peas and cover until bright green. In the meantime, brown pork in a skillet. Toss the quinoa with the pork, peas, feta, herbs, and almonds.

Puree all the dressing ingredients in the food processor. Toss the dressing with the salad ingredients. Season generously with salt and pepper. Serve tossed with fresh baby spinach.

Grapefruit, Spinach, Quinoa & Avocado Salad

Serves 2

Ingredients - Allergies: SF, GF, DF, EF, V, NF

- 1 cup red grapefruit
- 1/2 cup cooked
- 1 cup spinach
- 1/2 avocado

Dressing:
- 1 tbsp. oil or oil
- 1 tbsp. fresh lemon juice
- pinch of black pepper
- pinch of sea salt
- a pinch of dried basil

Instructions: Mix all ingredients.

Grilled Shrimp, Watermelon, Tomato & Spinach Salad

Serves 2

Ingredients - Allergies: SF, GF, EF, NF

- 1 cup grilled shrimps
- 1 cup chopped watermelon
- 1 cup arugula
- 1/2 cup cheese

Dressing:
- 1 tbsp. oil or black oil
- 1 tbsp. fresh lemon juice
- pinch of black pepper
- pinch of sea salt
- 1 tbsp. fresh basil

Instructions: Mix all ingredients.

Quinoa & Almond Superfoods Tabbouleh

Serves 2-3

Ingredients - Allergies: SF, GF, EF

- 2 cups cooked
- 1 bunch mint, leaves picked & 1 bunch flat leaf parsley
- 1/2 small red onion, finely chopped
- 1/4 Cup lemon juice& 1/4 Cup extra virgin oil
- 1/2 Cup whole almonds & 1/2 cup or sunflower seeds
- 1 Cup cherry tomatoes & 1 Avocado optional
- 1 Cup chopped Kale or Dandelion
- Low fat yogurt, to serve, optional

Instructions

Cook quinoa and let it cool. Chop off and discard half of the parsley stalks. Finely chop the remaining parsley bunch, mint and greens. Stir herbs in a salad bowl and add onion to drained quinoa. Combine lemon juice and olive oil and season well. Add other ingredients, mix and dress salad.

Kale, Avocado, Almond & Pomegranate Salad
Serves 2

Ingredients - Allergies: SF, GF, EF, V, DF, NF

- 1 cup kale
- 1/2 cup pomegranate seeds
- 1/2 cup chopped avocado
- 1/2 cup almonds
- 1/2 cup chopped orange

Dressing:
- 1 tbsp. oil
- 1 tbsp. fresh lemon juice
- pinch of black pepper
- pinch of sea salt
- 1 tbsp. seeds

Instructions: Mix all ingredients.

Quinoa, Green Peas, Asparagus & Radish Salad

Serves 2

Ingredients - Allergies: SF, GF, DF, EF, V, NF

- 1 cup cooked
- 1/2 cup chopped radish
- 1/2 cup blueberries
- 1 cup green peas mixed with seeds
- 1/2 cup asparagus

Dressing:
- 1 tbsp. oil or black oil
- 1 tbsp. fresh lemon juice
- pinch of black pepper
- pinch of sea salt

Instructions: Mix all ingredients.

Greek Cucumber Salad

Serves 2-3

Ingredients - Allergies: SF, GF, EF, NF

- 2-3 cucumbers, sliced
- 2 teaspoons salt
- 3 tbsp. lemon juice
- 1/4 tsp. paprika
- 1/4 tsp. white pepper
- 1/2 clove garlic, minced
- 4 fresh green onions, diced
- 1 cup thick Greek Yogurt
- 1/4 tsp. paprika

Instructions

Slice cucumbers thinly, sprinkle with salt and mix. Set aside for one hour. Mix lemon juice, water, garlic, paprika and white pepper, and set aside. Squeeze liquid from cucumber slices a few at a time, and place slices in the bowl. Discard liquid. Add lemon juice mixture, green onions, and yogurt. Mix and sprinkle additional paprika or dill over top. Chill for 1-2 hours.

Cucumber, Cilantro, Quinoa Tabbouleh

Serves 2

Ingredients - Allergies: SF, GF, DF, EF, NF, V

- 1 cup cooked mixed with 1 tbsp. sesame seeds
- 1/2 cup chopped tomato and green pepper
- 1 cup chopped cucumber
- 1/2 cup chopped cilantro

Dressing:
- 1 tbsp. oil
- 1 tbsp. fresh lemon juice
- pinch of black pepper
- pinch of sea salt

Instructions: Mix all ingredients.

Almond, Quinoa, Red Peppers & Arugula Salad

Serves 2

Ingredients - Allergies: SF, GF, DF, EF, NF, V

- 1 cup cooked mixed with 1 tbsp. pumpkin seeds
- 1/2 cup chopped almonds
- 1 cup chopped arugula
- 1/2 cup sliced red peppers

Dressing:
- 1 tbsp. oil or oil
- 1 tbsp. fresh lemon juice
- pinch of black pepper
- pinch of sea salt
- 1 tbsp. seeds

Instructions: Mix all ingredients.

Asparagus, Quinoa & Red Peppers Salad

Serves 2

Ingredients - Allergies: SF, GF, DF, EF, NF, V

- 1 cup cooked mixed with 1 tbsp. sunflower seeds
- 1 cup sliced red peppers
- 1 cup grilled asparagus
- Garnish with lime and parsley

Dressing:
- 1 tbsp. oil
- 1 tbsp. fresh lemon juice
- pinch of black pepper
- pinch of sea salt

Instructions: Mix all ingredients.

Chickpeas, Quinoa, Cucumber & Tomato Salad

Serves 2

Ingredients - Allergies: SF, GF, DF, EF, NF, V

- 1 cup cooked mixed with 1 tbsp. sesame seeds
- 1 cup cooked chickpeas
- 1 cup chopped cucumber and green onions
- 1/2 cup chopped tomato

Dressing:
- 1 tbsp. oil or black oil
- 1 tbsp. fresh lemon juice
- pinch of black pepper
- pinch of sea salt

Instructions: Mix all ingredients.

Quinoa, Spinach, Blueberries & Strawberries Salad

Serves 2

Ingredients - Allergies: SF, GF, DF, EF, V, NF

- 1 cup cooked mixed with 1 tbsp. ground seeds
- 1/2 cup strawberries
- 1/2 cup blueberries
- 1 cup spinach
- 1/2 chopped carrot

Dressing:
- 1 tbsp. oil
- 1 tbsp. fresh lemon juice
- pinch of black pepper
- pinch of sea salt
- a pinch of black cumin seeds

Instructions: Mix all ingredients.

Quinoa, Black Beans & Tomato Salad
Serves 2

Ingredients - Allergies: SF, GF, DF, EF, NF, V

- 1 cup cooked mixed with sesame seeds
- 1/2 cup tomato
- 1 cup Black beans
- 1/2 tbsp. fresh basil

Dressing:
- 1 tbsp. oil or oil
- 1 tbsp. fresh lemon juice
- pinch of black pepper
- pinch of sea salt
- 1 tbsp. seeds

Instructions: Mix all ingredients.

Pomegranate Avocado salad

Serves 1

Ingredients - Allergies: SF, GF, DF, EF, V

- 1 cup mixed greens, spinach, arugula, red leaf lettuce
- 1 ripe avocado, cut into 1/2-inch pieces
- 1/2 cup pomegranate seeds
- 1/4 cup pecan
- 1/4 cup blackberries
- 1/4 cup cherry tomatoes
- oil, salt, lemon juice

Instructions

Combine greens, pecan, cut avocado, tomatoes, pomegranates and blackberries in a salad bowl. Whisk together salt, olive oil and lemon juice and pour over salad.

Superfoods Reference Book

Unfortunately, I had to take out the whole Superfoods Reference Book out of all of my books because parts of that book are featured on my blog. I joined Kindle Direct Publishing Select program which allows me to have all my books free for 5 days every 3 months. Unfortunately, KDP Select program also means that all my books have to have unique content that is not available in any other online store or on the Internet (including my blog). I didn't want to remove parts of Superfoods Reference book that is already on my blog because I want that all people have free access to that information. I also wanted to be part of KDP Select program because that is an option to give my book for free to anyone. So, some sections of my Superfoods Reference Book can be found on my blog, under Superfoods menu on my blog. Complete Reference book is available for subscribers to my Superfoods Today Newsletter. Subscribers to my Newsletter will also get information whenever any of my books becomes free on Amazon. I will not offer any product pitches or anything similar to my subscribers, only Superfoods related information, recipes and weight loss and fitness tips. So, subscribe to my newsletter, download Superfoods Today Desserts free eBook which has complete Superfood Reference book included and have the opportunity to get all of my future books for free.

REFERENCES:

Morelli SA1, Torre JB, Eisenberger NI. The neural bases of feeling understood and not understood. Soc Cogn Affect Neurosci. 2014 Feb 14. [Epub ahead of print]

Oschman JL. Can electrons act as antioxidants? A review and commentary. J Altern Complement Med. 2007 Nov;13(9):955-67.

Ye L1, Guo J1, Ge RS2. Environmental pollutants and hydroxysteroid dehydrogenases. Vitam Horm. 2014;94:349-90. doi: 10.1016/B978-0-12-800095-3.00013-4.

Albuquerque TG1, Costa HS, Sanches-Silva A, Santos M, Trichopoulou A, D'Antuono F, Alexieva I, Boyko N, Costea C, Fedosova K, Karpenko D, Kilasonia Z, Koçaoglu B, Finglas P. Traditional foods from the Black Sea region as a potential source of minerals. J Sci Food Agric. 2013 Nov;93(14):3535-44. doi: 10.1002/jsfa.6164. Epub 2013 May 10.

Ali M1, Thomson M, Afzal M. Garlic and onions: their effect on eicosanoid metabolism and its clinical relevance. Prostaglandins Leukot Essent Fatty Acids. 2000 Feb;62(2):55-73.

Bornhoeft J1, Castaneda D, Nemoseck T, Wang P, Henning SM, Hong MY. The protective effects of green tea polyphenols: lipid profile, inflammation, and antioxidant capacity in rats fed an atherogenic diet and dextran sodium sulfate. J Med Food. 2012 Aug;15(8):726-32. doi: 10.1089/jmf.2011.0258. Epub 2012 Jun 25.

Ceylon Med J. 2014 Mar;59(1):4-8. doi: 10.4038/cmj.v59i1.6731.

Senadheera SP1, Ekanayake S, Wanigatunge C. Antioxidant potential of green leafy porridges.

Gülçin İ. Antioxidant activity of food constituents: an overview. Arch Toxicol. 2012 Mar;86(3):345-91. doi: 10.1007/s00204-011-0774-2. Epub 2011 Nov 20.

Heim KC1, Angers P, Léonhart S, Ritz BW. Anti-inflammatory and neuroactive properties of selected fruit extracts. J Med Food. 2012 Sep;15(9):851-4. doi: 10.1089/jmf.2011.0265. Epub 2012 Aug 7.

Meral O1, Alpay M, Kismali G, Kosova F, Cakir DU, Pekcan M, Yigit S, Sel T. Capsaicin inhibits cell proliferation by cytochrome c release in gastric cancer cells. Tumour Biol. 2014 Mar 30.

Moon JK1, Shibamoto T. Antioxidant assays for plant and food components. J Agric Food Chem. 2009 Mar 11;57(5):1655-66. doi: 10.1021/jf803537k.

Nagaraja P1, Aradhana N, Suma A, Shivakumar A, Chamaraja NA. Quantification of antioxidants by using chlorpromazine hydrochloride: application of the method to food and medicinal plant samples. Anal Sci. 2014;30(2):251-6.

Johnston C. Functional Foods as Modifiers of Cardiovascular Disease. Am J Lifestyle Med. 2009 Jul;3(1 Suppl):39S-43S.

Hernández-Ortega M1, Ortiz-Moreno A, Hernández-Navarro MD, Chamorro-Cevallos G, Dorantes-Alvarez L, Necoechea-Mondragón H. Antioxidant, antinociceptive, and anti-inflammatory effects of carotenoids extracted from dried pepper (Capsicum annuum L.). J Biomed Biotechnol. 2012;2012:524019. doi: 10.1155/2012/524019. Epub 2012 Oct 2.

Nicod N1, Chiva-Blanch G, Giordano E, Dávalos A, Parker RS, Visioli F. Green Tea, Cocoa, and Red Wine Polyphenols Moderately Modulate Intestinal Inflammation and Do Not Increase High-Density Lipoprotein (HDL) Production. J Agric Food Chem. 2014 Mar 12;62(10):2228-32. doi: 10.1021/jf500348u. Epub 2014 Mar 4.

Ownby SL, Fortuno LV, Au AY, Grzanna MW, Rashmir-Raven AM, Frondoza CG. (2014). Expression of pro-inflammatory mediators is inhibited by an avocado/soybean unsaponifiables and epigallocatechin gallate combination. J Inflamm (Lond). 2014 Mar 28;11(1):8.

Pastrana-Bonilla E1, Akoh CC, Sellappan S, Krewer G. Phenolic content and antioxidant capacity of muscadine grapes. J Agric Food Chem. 2003 Aug 27;51(18):5497-503.

Podsędek A1, Redzynia M1, Klewicka E2, Koziołkiewicz M1. Matrix effects on the stability and antioxidant activity of red cabbage anthocyanins under simulated gastrointestinal digestion. Biomed Res Int. 2014;2014:365738. doi: 10.1155/2014/365738. Epub 2014 Jan 19.

Seeram NP. Berry fruits: compositional elements, biochemical activities, and the impact of their intake on human health, performance, and disease. J Agric Food Chem. 2008 Feb 13;56(3):627-9. doi: 10.1021/jf071988k. Epub 2008 Jan 23.

Seeram NP1, Adams LS, Zhang Y, Lee R, Sand D, Scheuller HS, Heber D. Blackberry, black raspberry, blueberry, cranberry, red raspberry, and strawberry extracts inhibit growth and stimulate apoptosis of human cancer cells in vitro. J Agric Food Chem. 2006 Dec 13;54(25):9329-39.

Sharmin H1, Nazma S, Mohiduzzaman M, Cadi PB. Antioxidant capacity and total phenol content of commonly consumed selected vegetables of Bangladesh. Malays J Nutr. 2011 Dec;17(3):377-83.

Thomson SJ1, Rippon P, Butts C, Olsen S, Shaw M, Joyce NI, Eady CC. Inhibition of platelet activation by lachrymatory factor synthase (LFS)-silenced (tearless) onion juice.J Agric Food Chem. 2013 Nov 6;61(44):10574-81. doi: 10.1021/jf4030213. Epub 2013 Oct 22.

Your Free Gift

As a way of saying thanks for your purchase, I'm offering you my FREE eBook that is exclusive to my book and blog readers.

Superfoods Cookbook Book Two has over 70 Superfoods recipes and complements Superfoods Cookbook Book One and it contains Superfoods Salads, Superfoods Smoothies and Superfoods Deserts with ultra-healthy non-refined ingredients. All ingredients are 100% Superfoods.

It also contains Superfoods Reference book which is organized by Superfoods (more than 60 of them, with the list of their benefits), Superfoods spices, all vitamins, minerals and antioxidants. Superfoods Reference Book lists Superfoods that can help with 12 diseases and 9 types of cancer.

Other Books from this Author

Superfoods Today Diet is a Kindle Superfoods Diet that gives you 4 week Superfoods Diet meal plan as well as 2 weeks maintenance meal plan and recipes for weight loss success. It is an extension of Detox book and it's written for people who want to switch to Superfoods lifestyle.

Superfoods Today Body Care is a Kindle with over 50 Natural Recipes for beautiful skin and hair. It has body scrubs, facial masks and hair care recipes made with the best Superfoods like avocado honey, coconut, olive oil, oatmeal, yogurt, banana and Superfoods herbs like lavender, rosemary, mint, sage, hibiscus, rose.

Superfoods Today Cookbook is a Kindle that contains over 160 Superfoods recipes created with 100% Superfoods ingredients. Most of the meals can be prepared in under 30 minutes and some are really quick ones that can be done in 10 minutes only. Each recipe combines Superfoods ingredients that deliver astonishing amounts of antioxidants, essential fatty acids (like omega-3), minerals, vitamins, and more.

Superfoods Today Smoothies is a Kindle Superfoods Smoothies with over 70+ 100% Superfoods smoothies. Featured are Red, Purple, Green and Yellow Smoothies

Superfoods Today Salads is a Kindle that contains over 60 Superfoods Salads recipes created with 100% Superfoods ingredients. Most of the salads can be prepared in 10 minutes and most are measured for two. Each recipe combines Superfoods ingredients that deliver astonishing amounts of antioxidants, essential fatty acids (like omega-3), minerals, vitamins, and more.

Superfoods Today Kettlebells is a Kindle Kettlebells beginner's aimed at 30+ office workers who want to improve their health and build stronger body without fat.

Superfoods Today Red Smoothies is a Kindle Superfoods Smoothies with more than 40 Red Smoothies.

Superfoods Today 14 Days Detox is a Kindle Superfoods Detox that gives you 2 week Superfoods Detox meal plan and recipes for Detox success.

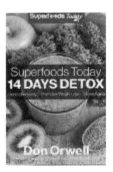

Superfoods Today Yellow Smoothies is a Kindle Superfoods Smoothies with more than 40 Yellow Smoothies.

Superfoods Today Green Smoothies is a Kindle Superfoods Smoothies with more than 35 Green Smoothies.

Superfoods Today Purple Smoothies is a Kindle Superfoods Smoothies with more than 40 Purple Smoothies.

Superfoods Cooking For Two is a Kindle that contains over 150 Superfoods recipes for two created with 100% Superfoods ingredients.

Nighttime Eater is a Kindle that deals with Nighttime Eating Syndrome (NES). Don Orwell is a life-long Nighttime Eater that has lost his weight with Superfoods and engineered a solution around Nighttime Eating problem. Don still eats at night✍. Don't fight your nature, you can continue to eat at night, be binge free and maintain low weight.

Superfoods Today Smart Carbs 20 Days Detox is a Kindle Superfoods that will teach you how to detox your body and start losing weight with Smart Carbs. The book has over 470+ pages with over 160+ 100% Superfoods recipes.

Superfoods Today Vegetarian Salads is a Kindle that contains over 40 Superfoods Vegetarian Salads recipes created with 100% Superfoods ingredients. Most of the salads can be prepared in 10 minutes and most are measured for two.

Superfoods Today Vegan Salads is a Kindle that contains over 30 Superfoods Vegan Salads recipes created with 100% Superfoods ingredients. Most of the salads can be prepared in 10 minutes and most are measured for two.

Superfoods Today Soups & Stews is a Kindle that contains over 70 Superfoods Soups and Stews recipes created with 100% Superfoods ingredients.

Superfoods Desserts is a Kindle Superfoods Desserts with more than 60 Superfoods Recipes.

Smoothies for Diabetics is a Kindle that contains over 70 Superfoods Smoothies adjusted for diabetics.

50 Shades of Superfoods for Two is a Kindle that contains over 150 Superfoods recipes for two created with 100% Superfoods ingredients.

50 Shades of Smoothies is a Kindle that contains over 70 Superfoods Smoothies.

50 Shades of Superfoods Salads is a Kindle that contains over 60 Superfoods Salads recipes created with 100% Superfoods ingredients. Most of the salads can be prepared in 10 minutes and most are measured for two. Each recipe combines Superfoods ingredients that deliver astonishing amounts of antioxidants, essential fatty acids (like omega-3), minerals, vitamins, and more.

Superfoods Vegan Desserts is a Kindle Vegan Dessert with 100% Vegan Superfoods Recipes.

Desserts **for Two** is a Kindle Superfoods Desserts with more than 40 Superfoods Desserts Recipes for two.

Superfoods Paleo Cookbook is a Kindle Paleo with more than 150 100% Superfoods Paleo Recipes.

Superfoods Breakfasts is a Kindle Superfoods with more than 40 100% Superfoods Breakfasts Recipes.

Superfoods Dump Dinners is a Kindle Superfoods with Superfoods Dump Dinners Recipes.

Healthy Desserts is a Kindle Desserts with more than 50 100% Superfoods Healthy Desserts Recipes.

Superfoods Salads in a Jar is a Kindle Salads in a Jar with more than 35 100% Superfoods Salads Recipes.

Smoothies for Kids is a Kindle Smoothies with more than 80 100% Superfoods Smoothies for Kids Recipes.

Vegan Cookbook for Beginners is a Kindle Vegan with more than 75 100% Superfoods Vegan Recipes.

Vegetarian Cooking for Beginners is a Kindle Vegetarian with more than 150 100% Superfoods Paleo Recipes.

Foods for Diabetics is a Kindle with more than 170 100% Superfoods Diabetics Recipes.

Made in United States
Troutdale, OR
12/09/2023